h to see Hungary

TIGERS AGAIN!

The Committee of the **RICHMOND FOOTBALL CLUB** is pleased to invite you to commence training under Senior Coach, Tom Hafey, at the Richmond Ground on Tuesday, February 1st, at 4.30 p.m.

CONGRATULATIONS KEVIN ON YOUR RECORD BREAKING DAY SATURDAY STOP ALL AT ADIDAS WISH YOU WELL AND ARE PROUD TO HAVE YOU IN OUR TEAM STOP GOOD LUCK IN THE FINALS STOP

REGARDS E.J.

WHAT A TIGER!

KEVIN'S MEDAL PLEA

F.L. PREMIERS

BARTLETT IS $1000 BEST

Tiger star cleaning up

Under 19 Grade
Footscray 11.12 d. Richmond 10.9
Best for **Footscray**: Madigan, Peters, Barrow, Barr, Shanahan, Taylor. **Goalkickers**: Hipwell 2, Madigan 2, Shanahan 2, Thorpe, Annett, Calder, Chivers, Barr.
Best for **Richmond**: Bartlett, Weston, Ronaldson, McLaren, Hoare, Dobson. **Goalkickers**: Weston 6, Parker, Davenport, Shiels, Ronaldson.

Richmond includes Strang, Bartlett

BRILLIANT BARTLETT STRIKES GOLD AGAIN

KB

FAMILIAR POSE: Celebrating a goal in my 350th game, against Melbourne in round 11, 1981. "Enthusiasm is catching," said Tom Hafey. "So is the lack of it."

A LIFE IN FOOTBALL

KEVIN BARTLETT
AS TOLD TO RHETT BARTLETT

Tribute by Kevin Sheedy
Foreword by Barry Richardson

QUITE A TASK: Breaking through the banner, the biggest made for a footy match, before my 400th game, in round 19, 1983. Note that my right foot got caught, causing me to trip.

I dedicate this book to my wife Denise
and our beautiful family for all their love and support.

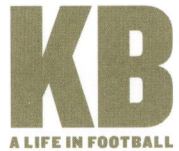

KB
A LIFE IN FOOTBALL

FOREWORD 14
By Barry Richardson

A TRIBUTE 22
By Kevin Sheedy

INTRODUCTION 32
By Rhett Bartlett

LEARNING THE GAME 36
Growing up in the shadows of Punt Road

PLAYING THE GAME 52
Premierships, milestones and captaincy capers

COACHING THE GAME 150
A dream job before my forced exit

WATCHING THE GAME 176
Behind the microphone and other adventures

AFTERWORD 214

CENTRE OF GREATNESS: It's people like these who made it possible for me to get the most out of my career. Here (from left) Graeme Bond, Kevin Sheedy, Mike Green, Tom Hafey, Merv Keane and Francis Bourke rally around me during the celebrations for my 200th game, in 1974.

LISTEN AND LEARN: Len Smith was a great football educator and strategist and my first senior coach at Richmond. Here he addresses us during a pre-season training session in 1965, my first senior year. I'm on the far left. Others include Daryl Beale (fourth from left), John Sheahan (fifth from left, with head bowed), John Perry (sixth from left), Bill Barrot (eighth from left), Owen Madigan (partially obscured by Smith), Ian Hayden (fourth from right), Alan 'Bull' Richardson (third from right), Neil Busse (second from right) and John Northey (far right). Note the blackboard at the far left with a Richmond team listed on it.

AMONG THE BEST: Bill Stephen, the then Fitzroy coach, addresses his Victorian squad players during a training session before my first state game, in 1968. The visible players are (from left) Darryl Gerlach (Essendon), Alex Jesaulenko (Carlton), Bob Skilton (South Melbourne), John Nicholls (Carlton), John Goold (Carlton), Denis Marshall (Geelong), Bill Barrot (Richmond), Ernie Hug (Collingwood), Hassa Mann (Melbourne), John Schultz (Footscray), Barry Davis (Essendon), Norm Brown (Fitzroy), Peter Hudson (Hawthorn), Stan Alves (Melbourne, obscured), me, Billy Goggin (Geelong) and John Sharrock (Geelong). Only a handful of us are wearing the jumpers of our League clubs.

ON THE FLY: Hawthorn wingman Alan Goad pressures me during a match at Glenferrie Oval in 1973.

FOREWORD
BY BARRY RICHARDSON

HUNGRY FOR SUCCESS

Kevin Bartlett the player was a standout for his speed and resourcefulness. His single-mindedness sometimes jeopardised team rules, but his loyalty was beyond reproach.

Any introduction to the life of Kevin Bartlett must deal with more than KB the brilliant footballer. He is one of life's interesting and at times enigmatic characters, evolving from simple beginnings to become a talented, rounded personality capable of mixing comfortably with prime ministers or paupers.

NEXT ONE: Our premiership chances under review in 1977.

In football and in life we can all tend towards having one year's experience ten times rather than the preferable ten years' experience, and Kevin's journey has definitely been the latter.

Look at what makes up the man: player, coach, commentator, after-dinner speaker, loyal friend, family man – you name it, and he has managed each part of his life with an admirable single-minded determination to not just succeed but to improve; simply to achieve the best he can in everything he attempts. So, was he always like this?

Those who knew him well in his early days at Tigerland would say the potential to be more than a great player was always there, manifested by a dry sense of humour mixed with a steely resolve.

I did not know KB all that well in my early years at Richmond, but when I came to play with him for some ten years I could sit back and admire from a front row seats as he constantly amazed us with his skills, his passion and his total approach to the game.

My indelible memory of KB the player is of speed, speed and more speed. You could not have caught him in a telephone box. If there was another standout quality, it was of his consistent level of excellence. KB never played bad games, only excellent, very good or good.

MOMENT TO SAVOUR: There is no better feeling in footy than just after a Grand Final victory. In this case, it's after the 1973 Grand Final. The injured Barry Richardson (left), Tom Hafey and I share our delight.

I played at full-back for some years with Bartlett as our first rover; from kick-outs I simply directed the ball to him whenever he had some space, knowing the ball would rarely come back.

When I was moved to full-forward it was not so good. The Tom Hafey style was to "just kick it high and long" and let the forwards get their own ball. KB's interpretation of the Hafey way was "if possible, kick it over your head for goal", so he could get the crumbs. I learned to lead to a miskick!

My respect for Kevin grew when I became his coach in 1977. I took over from Tom Hafey in controversial circumstances, having coached the reserves in 1976. I was 30 at the time, coaching players of my own age, former teammates, and champions like Francis Bourke, Kevin Sheedy, Royce Hart and KB. They had played all their football under Tommy, and KB in particular had a very close personal relationship with him.

Tommy's sacking – or forced resignation – affected his little mate deeply and I was uncertain how it would all unfold, particularly when I felt that some changes in the Hafey game plan were needed. I should not have worried. I received total support. Kevin's loyalty to me as an old teammate – now coach – was beyond reproach, and the fact that he

ALL FOR ONE: The Tigers do a lap of honour after winning the 1967 Grand Final. From left, Bill Barrot, Francis Bourke, Kevin Bartlett (partially obscured), Mike Patterson, Barry Richardson, Fred Swift (holding cup), John Perry (obscured), Paddy Guinane, Mike Perry, Graham Burgin, Royce Hart, John Ronaldson, Geoff Strang, Roger Dean, John Northey, Mike Green and Tony Jewell.

won the best-and-fairest in 1977 and was runner-up in 1978 bears testimony to his commitment to me and to his team and the club as a whole.

It is fair to say, though, that his single-minded approach to the way he played his game sometimes saw him outside team rules; i.e. the convention of using handball as a first thought rather than as a second (or in KB's mind, third or fourth) was never part of KB's game plan.

Like him and respect as I do, it is not my intention to canonise him as St Kevin. If he made one mistake in his football journey it was not to understand that there are only two types of coaches, those who have been sacked and those about to be sacked. Whereas loyalty to his friends and teammates has been a defining quality, many of us were a trifle bemused by his long disappearance from the club that had shaped his life and profile. We are all delighted that he's back, and has re-embraced this great club.

Even though our playing days are long over, strong memories remain and various recognitions that come our way mean much more if celebrated by former teammates and peers.

I once wrote in *The Sunday Age*, that I had been greatly affected on being inducted into Richmond's Hall of Fame – it was a humbling experience.

I fantasised on that happy occasion that I could create my own Team of Dreams, with me being welcome to kick the footy around with deceased champions such as Barney Herbert, Roy Wright, Max Oppy and the legendary Jack Dyer.

Other Hall of Famers such as Bill Barrot, Royce Hart, Francis Bourke, Michael Green, Kevin Sheedy, Ian Stewart and Neil Balme would be part of it as well, with KB enjoying the spoils that would flow from this wonderful bunch.

I note there is one significant anomaly in this book. It is a photo of Kevin Bartlett doing press-ups with Sheedy and Bourke. One look at those arms will verify that KB never did a press-up in his life. Perhaps he was so quick and so good he never needed to.

Barry Richardson, April 2011

Barry Richardson and Kevin Bartlett were teammates in three premiership teams, in 1967, 1969 and 1974, and they played in the same teams on 117 occasions, from 1965 to 1974. KB played under Richardson as coach for two seasons, 1977-78. His record in those seasons was 25 games and 99 goals.

VICTORY PARADE: 1. Royce Hart leads the Tigers after our victory over North Melbourne in the 1974 Grand Final. Others include 2: Barry Richardson. 3: Alan Schwab. 4: Terry Phelan (photographer). 5: Ray Jamieson (photographer). 6: Bill Tindale (photographer). 7: Kevin Sheedy. 8: David Thorpe. 9: Gareth Andrews (arms aloft). 10: Paul Sproule. 11: Mike Green. 12: Kevin Morris (hands on head). 13: Brian Roberts. 14: John Murie (photographer). 15: Kevin Bartlett. 16: Merv Keane. 17: Daryl Cumming. 18: David Cloke (obscured). 19: Francis Bourke. 20: Dick Clay (No.2). 21: Wayne Walsh (arms aloft). 22: Peter Power (fitness instructor in tracksuit). 23: Bill Boromeo (bald trainer). 24: Neil Busse. 25: Robbie McGhie. 26: Allan Cooke 27: George McHutchison (statistician) 28: Col Saddington (reserves coach, arms around Hafey). 29: Tom Hafey. 30: Neil Balme. 31: Cameron Clayton (bare torso). 32: Barry Davis. 33: Ron Barassi. 34: David Robb. 35: Barry Cable. 36: John Rantall. 37: Doug Wade. 38: Sam Kekovich. 39: Max Ritchie. 40: Keith Greig. 41: Wayne Schimmelbusch.

CAPTAIN BLOOD: Jack Dyer, in his inimitable style, congratulates me on breaking his Richmond club record of 310 games in 1979. Jack's games tally was later upgraded to 312 when a couple of extra games were found.

A TRIBUTE
BY KEVIN SHEEDY

ENDURING FRIENDSHIP

Kevin Sheedy and Kevin Bartlett have been lifelong friends, starting as young school mates and later as teammates in the most successful Richmond side of all time.

When Kevin and I were kids, he was such a lot of fun. He could call the Melbourne Cup or discuss any sport and the men and women who played them. We were only 10 or 12 then and he could make us laugh in that era just after World War II when we had to make our own entertainment.

As I write this tribute, I think of that young boy, and I think of the man he has become – a football icon, and now one of the bests sports commentators in Australia. What a wonderful football career he had. These statistics tell it all.

His 403 games for Richmond featured:
- five premierships
- five best-and-fairest awards
- leading goalkicker four times
- one Norm Smith Medal
- while successfully completing one handball.

We've all dined out on that final statistic of Kevin's for years, if only because it was true!

But as with all great sports people, there is a lot more to KB than sheer statistics.

His is the story of a young boy who had a dream to play in the VFL and the talent, and the commitment, to make it happen.

In my memoir, *Stand Your Ground*, I described the two of us as the Keith Richards and Mick Jagger of football. We go right back to the schoolyard at Prahran Tech College, and also the Try Boys Club in Cromwell Road, South Yarra. As I was preparing myself to play senior footy, Kevin was always my measuring stick: how was I going against him?

While I was on my 'scenic' route to the VFL via the VFA, I kept looking at what Kevin was doing with Richmond and thinking to myself, 'Well I know he is a better player than me, but if I work as hard as he does, well maybe there is a place for me, too, with Richmond.' The distance between Prahran and Richmond is only six kilometres but the challenge was enormous. When I finally got to Punt Road, it was just a thrill to be in the same side as him. When I arrived, he was still drifting between the

THREE WINNERS: The article (top) describes how Francis Bourke, Kevin Sheedy and I were hoping to play in another premiership together; the telegram that 'Sheeds' sent me for my 300th game.

FOR LIFE: I first met Kevin Sheedy when we were primary school students and we've continued our friendship ever since.

firsts and the seconds and there was a bit of talk about that he was too skinny to make it. Too skinny! Where were these people looking? He had calves the size of rock melons, and he was as hard as rock.

The doubters were proven entirely wrong by all that followed – the first player to reach 400 games, his brilliance in big games, his consistency.

Without a doubt, Kevin was the absolute superstar of my time at Richmond. And when you consider who else was in the side at that time, that's a big statement. We had the self-appointed centre half-forward of the century, Royce Hart, in our side, not to mention Ian Stewart, who won a Brownlow Medal at both St Kilda and Richmond. And Francis Bourke. Each of these three Richmond players made it into the official AFL Team of the Century. Strangely the name Kevin Bartlett, for all his achievements, was missing.

I still ask the question: Why?

By the time of his retirement, Kevin was a club legend. And why not? Even at the end of his career, when banished to the forward-line, he still kicked more than 80 goals in a season, maybe the only small forward to do so.

But that's Kevin the footballer, always doing it better than everyone else. If I reflect on Kevin Bartlett, the person, rather than Kevin Bartlett, the footballer, I would like to say that he has been one of the absolute superstars among my friends over the years. When he walks into a room, it just seems to light up. Our friendship is built on trust and loyalty. Kevin and I have long made it a policy to always tell each other the truth.

Our conversations are as easy now as they were all those years ago in and around Cromwell Road. In fact it's just been a continuous conversation – about footy, about life, about friendships.

One of the reasons I have written as many books about football as I have is to provide information and inspiration to the next generations coming into the game. The *500 Club*, which featured all the great coaches, was to be the textbook I never had when I took up coaching. A book about the life and times

about Kevin Bartlett just has to be the best textbook for anyone wanting to play our Australian game at the highest level. It is a must read. Kevin's life from those early days in the inner suburbs of Melbourne, to premiership player, to become one of the best broadcasters in Australian sport, should inspire every young Australian, just as he used to inspire the

VITAL VETERANS: With Kevin Sheedy (left) and Francis Bourke at pre-season training in 1979. The three of us went on to coach and become members of the Australian Football Hall of Fame. Francis and I played in five premierships together, and I shared three with Sheeds. We played a total of 954 games for the Tigers!

young Kevin John Sheedy and his mates in the crazy days hurtling around Princes Park, Prahran.

KB, thanks for the honour of being asked to write this tribute, and thanks for everything else you have given to me, and to hundreds of thousands of your fellow Australians, and to our wonderful Australian game.

Kevin Sheedy, April 2011

Kevin Sheedy and Kevin Bartlett played a total of 654 games for Richmond, and were teammates in three premiership teams, in 1969, 1973 and 1974. They played in the same teams on 240 occasions, from 1967 to 1979.

FALLEN HERO: This is before my 400th game. "Running through the banner was like running through a brick wall," I said at the time.

	1ST	2ND	3RD
3	3	1	2

WITH GUSTO: President Neville Crowe (left) and I belt out the Tigers' stirring theme song after defeating Melbourne in a high-scoring game in round 19, 1988. The score was 23.11 (149) to 20.11 (131).

LONELY TIMES: It's a long walk back to the rooms after a 10-goal loss to Fitzroy in round 20, 1991, and there's not much sympathy from the faces in the crowd. Looking back, it was the day that sealed my dismissal.

BIG BOOTS: Would Rhett become a Tiger like his Dad? I never put any pressure on him to do so.

INTRODUCTION
BY RHETT BARTLETT

MY DAD THE CHAMPION

I grew up at Punt Road, cadging chewy from the trainers, watching the champions training late into the evening, and sitting with the stats men on match days.

I never saw my father play League football. I was born in 1979, so I was just four years old when my old man took the field for his 403rd and final game. Yet so many of my memories of Dad while I was growing up involve football. I can pinpoint the exact date of so many occasions because, more often that not, they were photographed by the press.

There I am at my Dad's feet, 'Pageboy Rhett', as *The Herald* proclaimed, yelling out to the Moomba crowd as my father towered above me with a sceptre and crown. Truth be told, I was screaming because the sceptre was too heavy for Dad to hold. He kept losing his grip and it kept hitting me on the head.

Or there's the lovely photo taken on the back porch of our family home, with the two of us tying the bootlaces of my footy boots. It was one of the media's early attempts to suggest that I would try to follow in my father's footsteps and play League football. But I never did want to follow in his footsteps. Instead I found a greater interest in playing tennis. Dad never once complained. I'm sure he was a little disappointed, but he never spoke to me about it and he never pressured me to play football.

I now say that Dad played enough games of football for all our family, so there was no need for me to add to the tally. When my father was appointed coach of Richmond in late 1987, I was eight. On many days during the week he would pick me up after school and take me with him to training at Punt Road. Before long I became part of the furniture.

I can still remember running around the old ground as it got dark. I recall often asking the veteran trainer 'Dusty' O'Brien for a single piece of chewing gum or a drink of cordial. I would sit in on selection meetings in the coach's room, which was nothing more than a desk and some strange, tiered seating with carpet all over it.

READY TO GO: It's 1982 and Rhett and I are looking forward to the new season.

KING AND HEIR: One of the joys of being the 1984 King of Moomba (top) was having Rhett along for the ride. Here are also some of the family's footy mementoes.

I remember watching Jeff Hogg, Michael Roach, Mark Lee, Jim Jess, Matthew Knights and Brendon Gale at training. In particular, I closely followed my childhood hero, Trent Nichols. One year I had a haircut that quite resembled Trent's, which my father pointed out, much to my embarrassment and no doubt Trent's, at an annual general meeting.

Game day was even more fun. We would get to the ground very early to watch the reserves match, and I would take my seat in the stand among the Richmond statisticians. In the late 1980s, statistics were collected on one large sheet lovingly crafted with multiple coloured pens. There was not a computer to be seen. How times have changed.

As the siren sounded after senior games at the MCG, I would race down to the fence and wait for Dad to walk past. When I saw him, I would jump up and down, wave my hands, yell out... anything to grab his attention. If he saw me (the success rate was about 80 per cent), he would ask the policeman who was accompanying him if I could come on to the ground. They never said no. So most matches ended up with me walking up the race with my father. I recall one game in which the Tigers were thrashed by Geelong. As we approached the race, supporters were spitting at the players and Dad. I will always remember Dad grabbing my shirt collar and pulling me in closer. I felt safe.

I have so many memories. Another is the Save Our Skins campaign. My sister Cara and I stood in front of the MCG rattling tins. One man came up to us and plonked down a large container of coins that he had just won at the pokies. We gave them to life member Alice Wills, who took them to Punt Road the following morning to be counted.

I remember watching the team at Monash University on a night when a huge hailstorm hit, prompting the entire playing squad to squeeze into a tiny changing room. I remember staying back very late one night at training, sitting in the car with the lights on, watching as Barry Young tried to hit the goalpost with set shots. (It was a training drill designed to improve kicking accuracy.)

MR CHIPS: What do you do when you've just been announced as Richmond coach? You do what you've always done on a Friday evening: tuck into a feed of fish and chips with the family. There's Rhett, 8, Sharna, 14, Denise, and Cara, 12. It's a night late in 1987.

Not every memory is a happy one. I often think back to the afternoon I came home from school and learned that the club had ended Dad's coaching career. There he was, standing near the doorway, waiting for me to arrive, his arms open, asking for a hug.

"Mate, I got sacked today," he said, squeezing me tightly. "I just want to thank you for all your support."

It was the first time I saw Dad cry.

It may sound strange, but it took until the AFL centenary year of 1996 for me to finally understand the role that Dad had played in football. There he was, at the inaugural Hall of Fame induction accepting his plaque. There I was, front and centre taking a photo. I felt so proud to be his son.

Come to think of it, I've been very lucky to have followed Dad around during his time as coach and also during his time in the media. I've been blessed to be sitting alongside him for many of football's finest moments: Jason Dunstall's 17 goals against Richmond, the 1000th career goal of Gary Ablett, the last game at Moorabbin, E.J. Whitten's final lap of honour, the first game at Docklands, the Brisbane Lions' three consecutive premierships... I could go on.

This publication is an oral and pictorial history of my father's career. In his own words, he sets the record straight on his memories of growing up, his time at Richmond, the friendships he has made in the media, and the unforgettable memories he created for everyone who follows our game.

Australian Football is a beautiful creation. In my case, it's a game that underpins the love of a father and his son. It's hard not to get emotional when I walk with my father into the MCG, the ground where he went with *his* father to watch Footscray win the 1954 Grand Final.

I often catch myself thinking of that moment as we approach the stadium, and how football has been a dear friend to Dad for all these years.

Rhett Bartlett, April 2011

KB

LEARNING THE GAME

RARE PHOTO: A young KB about to handball on Richmond's Punt Road Oval.

FIRST OF MANY: Schoolmates at Hawksburn State School raise me on their shoulders after the school had won the lightning premiership trophy for the district.

KB
LEARNING THE GAME

DREAMING OF THE BIG TIME

A childhood spent kicking paper footballs in Richmond parks evolved to a place in the Tigers' under-age teams before a move into the senior team in 1965.

My mother and my grandparents came from Footscray and my godparents came from Yarraville, so we were a strong Footscray family. Herb Henderson, full-back in the Bulldogs' only premiership team was my favourite player. Every time we went to the MCG we always sat right on the wing in the Southern Stand.

We went to the 1954 Grand Final and I can remember seeing Charlie Sutton lead the team out, he had big bandages on his thighs. Mum was crying with joy after the final siren and somehow that night we finished at the Footscray Town Hall, which was floodlit as they introduced the players. I would have been wearing my Footscray gear with Henderson's No.25 on the back, with the red, white and blue socks and beanie as well.

My father worked in South Yarra at Berkowitz Furniture. We had an old blue Ford Zephyr, which was a step up from our previous car, a Ford Prefect, and the motorbike and sidecar that preceded the cars. In those days, Mum and I would sit in the sidecar and given there were no seatbelts, I would sit on her lap. I went to Hawksburn State School because we first lived in South Yarra, at 285 Malvern

GOOD TIMES: That's me in front with Dad, Charlie, and my sister Pat; horsing around; me at three years of age.

CHAMPIONS OF TOMORROW: The Prahran Tech footy team, with me in the front row holding the footy. Below is an array of my schoolboy trophies. The bottom trophy is the first I ever won. It was the Hawksburn State School's best-and-fairest award, which I won in grade four.

Road where the Housing Commission flats are today. I lived there with my parents and my two sisters Pat and Val.

There were shop fronts leading all the way up Commercial Road, from the corner of Chapel Street to Williams Road, and we lived behind a boot-making shop, about 200 metres from Hawksburn State School.

When I finished Grade Six it was decided I would go to a technical school, and the closest to us was Prahran Tech. Unfortunately the owners of the bootmaking shop expanded, and we had to vacate the room we were in out the back.

We moved to 189 Lennox St Richmond, which was a big but dilapidated boarding house. We had only one room and a little kitchenette, which my parents thought was large enough. There were shared toilets, washrooms and bathrooms. An old lady owned it. She used to come around and knock every Thursday and ask for the rent and Mum would give her the money. There was no grass in the backyard, just gravel, as well as five or six bungalows and community kitchens.

In Year Seven, I used to catch the No. 77 tram from Swan Street over the Yarra River and down Chapel Street all the way to High Street, which is where the school was.

If you were a typical boy at the time, you would come home every day after school, see your Mum and then go straight across to a park and play there until it got dark. Kids would just meet there. Sometimes I had a football. We used to play a lot of paper football; you could kick this combination of tightly rolled-up newspaper and rubber bands a fair way. Even in the schoolyard we played most of the time with a paper footy.

You'd roll up and generally start up a match. The goalposts were two trees at one end and you would throw your jumpers down at other end to mark the other goals. Some people say I used to sell newspapers. Truth be told, that's not correct, but I did help people who sold newspapers.

Kevin Sheedy lived in Prahran opposite the old Jam Factory in Chapel Street. He would come down to the local park with his brother Pat. They were just a couple of the kids who would turn up. Kevin used to sell newspapers near the Jam Factory and I had friends who used to sell on the corner of Commercial Road and Chapel Street in front of Read's department store. I used to stand on the corners with them and help them sell a few papers. I didn't actually have a paper round of my own.

I left school in Year 10, or Intermediate as it was then known, after my mother saw an ad from the PMG (the Postmaster General Department was the Government-owned forerunner of Telstra and Australia Post) stating that it was looking for apprentices. She sent a letter on my behalf and I got a position as an apprentice instrument-maker, helping to make electro-mechanical instruments like volt meters, amp meters and temperature

WELL TURNED OUT: The 1961 form-three class from Prahran Tech. That's me in the back row, seventh from the left, with my torso tilted. At right is an article that claimed I was sick of winning trophies. Never!

GIFTED RUNNER: As a young footballer, I tested myself in another field by following Victoria's professional running circuit. This is a heat of the 100-yards event at Stawell in 1964. I am on the far left.

THEY'RE OFF: This is Graeme Bond (left) and me practising our starts under Bill Boromeo, who was also our junior footy coach at Richmond.

gauges. At a later date I was appointed to the PMG's research laboratories.

I did my training at the PMG workshops in South Melbourne, behind the old Prince Henry's Hospital, and that's where I learned fitting and turning and all sorts of other mechanical things. They also had an instrumentation shop where you had to repair the electrical instruments. I was required to go to school for one day a week for five years at RMIT to do the instrumentation course. The Try Boys Society was a youth club in South Yarra just up from Hawksburn State School. I played footy for the Try Boys until I heard that Richmond had an under-17 team, so I thought I would go down to the club and ask for a game.

It must have been early February and I just walked to the club at Punt Road and knocked on the door. Bill Boromeo, the coach of the under-17s, answered the door. He had me lift a few weights and then told me to come back in about five weeks when the pre-season training formally began.

Bill's father was Bert Boromeo, a great Carlton player in the 1920s who later played for Richmond, so the family had strong ties to the Tigers. Bill encouraged me to get a clearance from the Try Boys so I could play for the Richmond under-17s.

But there was a complication: the Try Boys played in the Caulfield-Oakleigh District Football League, which hated losing players to other competitions. I didn't have a permit to play when the season began. For the first two weeks I ran the boundary.

TRUE BLUE: A selection of the sashes won under Bill's coaching. Graeme won a Maryborough Gift while I won the 1968 Portland sprint double, the 120 yards and 75 yards events.

TOP CUBS: This is the Richmond under-17 team in 1962. I'm in the front row, on the right, next to Bill Boromeo.

Soon afterwards we played Collingwood fourths and we had a few injuries, so Bill played me as a rover under his son's name. Then Maurie Fleming, who was the president of Richmond, somehow got a clearance for me and I was then able to play under my own name. I was 15 at the time.

Michael Green played in the under-17s and became a lifelong friend. Bill Walford was another under-17 player who went on to play senior football for Richmond.

Collingwood, Hawthorn and Melbourne also had under-17 teams and I can remember one of the games against Collingwood at Clifton Hill. Graeme 'Jerker' Jenkin was playing and he was the biggest man I had ever seen in my life. I think we used to play Hawthorn at Box Hill, while our home games were played at Punt Road on Saturday mornings immediately before the under-19s. Graeme Richmond was the coach of the under-19s in 1962.

I had a good year in 1962 and won the under-17s' best and fairest and the goalkicking. They had an end of season night, at Kanis's

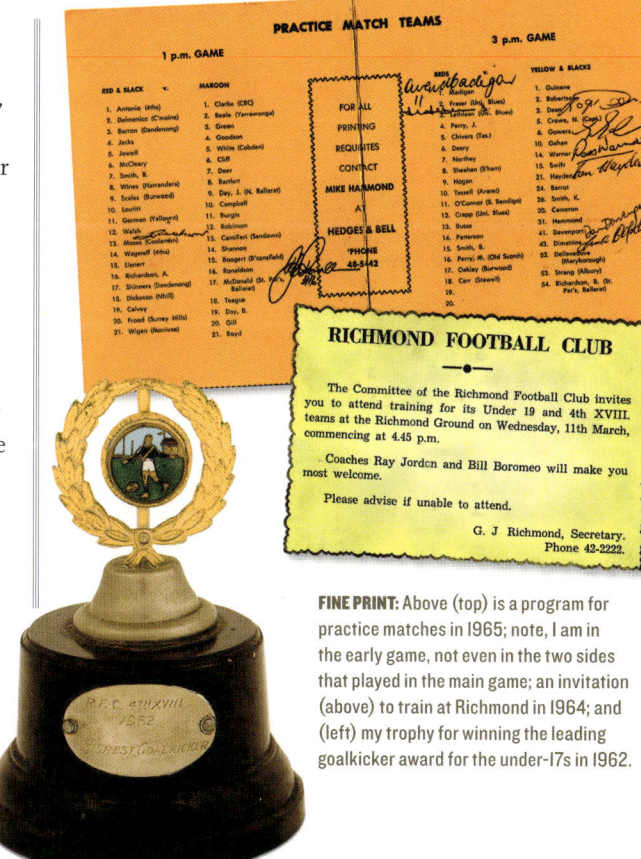

FINE PRINT: Above (top) is a program for practice matches in 1965; note, I am in the early game, not even in the two sides that played in the main game; an invitation (above) to train at Richmond in 1964; and (left) my trophy for winning the leading goalkicker award for the under-17s in 1962.

Café on Bridge Road, Richmond, which Bill organised. Richmond senior players Des Rowe and Ron Branton presented the trophies, which gave us a tremendous thrill.

Graeme Richmond was no longer the coach of the under-19s in 1963 because he had taken on the role of club secretary. Ray Jordon was brought in as coach and I was elevated to the under-19s — even though I was still eligible for the under 17s — because Richmond had told me there were "great opportunities" for rovers at the club at the time as long as I "trained hard and remained conscientious".

Jordon was loud and forceful and quite a taskmaster. I can remember his voice bellowing across the ground. I can't specifically remember him swearing at the players but he used to go crook at the umpire a fair bit. He was a good teacher of the game. We made the finals in 1963 and I played in the centre because Barry Teague was the rover. My first final was against Geelong and I lasted all of about three seconds. The opening bounce was crooked, the ball went backwards, I moved towards it then someone came in from the side and knocked me to the ground.

I couldn't stand up and my right hip was really painful. The trainers got me to my feet and carried me down to the forward pocket but I couldn't put any weight on my leg. They carried me from the field and into the rooms. I lay on trestle table and an ambulance was called.

And so I was to meet Jack Dyer. I looked up from the trestle table and there he was. He asked me how I was going and gave me words of encouragement such as "You will be okay" and "You'll get over this quickly." It was just fantastic of him to come into the rooms and speak to someone he didn't know. My admiration for Jack started from that day.

The ambulance took me to the Prince Henry's Hospital, where I finally caught up with my parents. They had missed the start of the match and spent the first quarter scanning the ground trying to find me. I was still lying in hospital an hour later when they wheeled in my teammate Frank Dimattina, who had been concussed.

The initial diagnosis was that I had a broken my pelvis but the doctors took X-rays and there was a shadow on my right hip. It emerged that I had a cyst on my hip, which I may have been born with, but which had to be removed. I was in hospital for two weeks after the surgery and it left me with a 30-centimetre gash from my kidneys to my thigh. The scar is still quite visible today.

My compensation for the incident was winning the under-19 best and fairest for that season. I was still only 16.

The following season, 1964, was a year of rehabilitation, because I was very tender in my hip, back and groin areas. I still played a bit of football

MORE ACCOLADES: Another article and another trophy, with a potted history of my year in the under-19 team in 1963. Note that they had a column for kicks but not handballs.

ON THE BALL: Peter Hogan and I were good friends and yet rivals for a roving position when this picture was taken in 1966. Peter played 40 games for the Tigers before becoming a prominent VFA footballer and a very successful businessman.

GOOD WORK: Class mates check out my reward for winning the RMIT apprentice-of-the-year award for making instruments.

EARLY DAYS: The *Football Record* (top) from my first senior game, against St Kilda in round three 1965; my first senior membership card, in 1965; the invitation to train under Tom Hafey in 1966.

including one game at centre half-forward in the under-17s in which I kicked 10 goals.

It was the reserves' policy to have an under-19s player sit on the bench in case they were short a player, and I did that for one game against Collingwood at Punt Road. I actually got on the ground with three minutes to go. I then ran off the ground and the team manager drove me to Victoria Park where I sat on the bench for the under 19s before coming on late in the game.

For most of 1964 I played in the under-19s. We won our first final, against North Melbourne, by 14 points. The preliminary final was against Melbourne. I played the first half at full-forward and then was switched into the centre. We lost by three goals.

In 1965 I played some practice matches in the reserves. I must have gone okay because I was on the tram home from work one day when I saw a headline in the paper suggesting a young Tiger recruit would be a shock selection for that weekend's final practice match. I wondered who this recruit was.

When I got home there was a telegram that read: *"You have been selected to play in the main practice game on the MCG, please bring your boots ..."*

So I turned up to the practice game and was handed a new pair of socks by legendary Richmond property steward Charlie Callander. I kicked three goals while playing as a changing rover with Peter Hogan and Frank Dimattina.

I played the first two games of 1965 in the reserves and while I played well I had no inkling of what was ahead. When senior coach Len Smith called me over at training on the Thursday night to tell me I would be 19th man that weekend against St Kilda, I was initially disappointed because I thought he was talking about the reserves.

Len asked why I wasn't happy. I said, 'I thought I probably played okay in the first two games and therefore I thought I would get a game.'

Len congratulated me and assured me I would be playing in the seniors. I got dressed after training and raced home to tell my parents the good news. They were sceptical, even though it was Len Smith who had told me the news.

So we just waited until 9pm to switch on the radio and hear Ron Casey, Lou Richards and Allan Nash read out the League teams. When it came to Richmond, it was Kevin Bartlett as 19th man and Trevor Gowers as 20th man. And that's how it all started.

At half-time, I remember Len Smith saying to me, "Just be patient, you will get on," and not long before three-quarter time I got my opportunity.

Sadly, my first game was Len's last game as coach because he had a heart attack the following Monday. I was at work when I heard. Len didn't coach Richmond again. He was replaced by Jack Titus, who narrowly missed out on coaching the Tigers to the finals in 1965. Len passed away in 1967 before we had won the Grand Final.

YELLOW AND BLACK: The Richmond team from round eight, 1965. The bow-tied coach is Jack 'Skinny' Titus. I am front row, second from left, about to play my sixth game of League football. Four players from this team would coach Richmond. The others were: Tony Jewell (back row, second from left), Mike Patterson (back row, fifth from left) and John Northey (middle row, far left).

In 1965 I played my first game against St Kilda in round three. The following week I remember going to the game with my parents on the train. We played at Windy Hill. I lined up on Alec Epis – 'The Kookaburra' – and kicked my first goal. I was playing in a forward pocket, changing rover with Frank Dimattina.

As second rover, I spent about 30 per cent of the time on the ball. It was a great learning experience for me as I was still frail, having done no weight training. I was just a young skinny 18-year-old playing League football. I played 14 out of 18 games in 1965 so I was very pleased with my debut year.

I was probably given games I didn't deserve. The coach, Skinny Titus, probably saw a bit of a future in me and gave me a few chances, but it was only in round 15 and 16 that I was dropped back down to the reserves. In 1966 Tommy Hafey came to the club and that's when training started to get tough. He toughened a lot of us up and made the Tigers physically stronger.

Richmond played Carlton at Princes Park in the first game of the year. Tommy sat on the bench for his first game as coach and I was 19th man, so I sat beside him. My memories are that I drove Tommy mad, wanting to get on the ground. Tommy likes to remind me that I kept saying 'Get that player off, put me on.'

MAN IN A SUIT: The official Richmond club blazer in the late 1960s.

Peter Hogan got knocked down and struggled from then on, so I did get on the ground. The interesting thing about that first game of 1966 was that the siren didn't sound to end the game. The umpire found out the game was over when a policeman on a horse galloped onto the ground to inform the umpire that the siren had sounded.

I must have really annoyed Tommy on the bench that day, because he dropped me to the reserves the following week.

The turning point of my career was round 15, 1966, when Richmond played Collingwood at the MCG. I was on the bench again. During the first quarter, the Tigers' Paddy Guinane accidently knocked out Frank Dimattina.

The Age newspaper reported that 'Guinane, charging forward, cannoned off Mick Erwin and flattened Dimattina so thoroughly he had to be taken off.' I was sent on the field as rover, and ended up kicking two goals.

The next week I was picked to play on a wing against Geelong at the MCG. My opponent was Tony Polinelli. Frank played against Geelong but was still feeling the effect of the knock so he missed the final two games of the season. I played first rover in those games and they proved my launching pad into 1967.

I played the practice matches of 1967 as rover and from then on I was picked as Richmond's first rover.

In hindsight, I owe my roving career to the misfortune of Frank Dimattina. Frank and I played in the under-19s together and we were very close friends – we still are. Frank was a very good player; he played on Bob Skilton in his first match and was the Tigers' best on that day. But he never fully recovered from the accident with Paddy Guinane. That left Peter Hogan, the gun recruit from Portland, and me as the roving combination.

It was an odd season for the club in 1966. We lost only four games out of 18 but still missed out on making the four. Here we were on 13½ wins, having drawn with North Melbourne, boasting a percentage of 123.2 and we couldn't even make the finals!

BETWEEN HAWKS: I battle with Hawthorn's Peter Crimmins (left) and Peter Chilton at Glenferrie Oval in the late 1960s.

KB
PLAYING THE GAME

FINEST HOUR: The great Ron Barassi presents me with the Norm Smith Medal after the 1980 Grand Final. I was honoured to be the first Richmond player to receive the medal.

KB
PLAYING THE GAME

1967 GRAND FINAL

My first Grand Final was an epic thriller against Geelong, full of brilliant individual acts and tense moments at the finish.

Fred Swift, the great Richmond player and our captain in 1967 was going through a form slump and there was a lot of talk about him perhaps being dropped from the side on the way to the finals. He had been playing a bit on the half-forward flank and as a ruck-rover because the club felt he was a bit small to play full-back, particularly against a player such as Geelong's Doug Wade, who he would likely be up against in the finals.

During the year, Mick Erwin played at full-back although Fred had a stronger and more reliable kicking style than Mick. So despite Swift's form slump, Tom Hafey didn't like the idea of dropping the captain as we made our way into the finals. Yet on the eve of the finals campaign Swift was out of the side! The committee had decided he should be dropped. But the more Tommy thought about it, the more he felt that would be too disruptive to the group, so Tom moved Fred back to full-back and unfortunately for Mick, he missed out on playing in any of the final matches that year.

And the rest, as they say, is history. Fred played a tremendous finals series, holding his own against Doug Wade in the Grand Final, and taking one of the most controversial marks in a premiership, an overhead mark deep in defence that Geelong fans claim he took over the goal line, but which Richmond fans naturally argue he took right on

MEMORIES OF 1967: The clipping is from round 12, 1967. I kicked two goals but the Tigers lost to Essendon. We then won our next eight games to snare the flag.

LEADERS OF '67: Captain Fred Swift and coach Tom Hafey grasp the cup.

RIPPER, ROYCE: Royce Hart soars to take his famous mark over the Cats defender Peter Walker in the last quarter of the 1967 Grand Final. Bill Brown has the best view. Note the near absence of players around the ball, a marked contrast to what happens in the modern game.

the goal line. After taking the mark, Fred simply played on straight away and kicked a lovely drop kick deep out of defence. For me, the 1967 Grand Final holds some great memories. I kicked 778 goals in my career, but I reckon the best of them was on that afternoon.

It was late in the last quarter, and there was less than a goal in it, when the ball came loose near the goals and five players converged on it. We all got there at once, but I got my hands on the football first, ran backwards out of the pack, turned around and kicked the goal that sealed the Grand Final.

All up, I kicked three goals in the game, including the first and last goals of the final quarter. I was rewarded with my name in the paper as one of the best players. Other memories I have of the drought-breaking premiership included how Bill Barrot dominated in the centre, roamed all around the ground and contributed a very important goal.

Royce Hart took one of the most famous Grand Final marks over Geelong's Peter Walker, while John Ronaldson's goal from the MCC members' side, from a long, long way out may be the greatest drop-kick goal ever in a Grand Final. He was in the side only because Neville Crowe was unfairly rubbed out for striking John Nicholls. Ronaldson then kicked another difficult goal from the other side of the ground.

Richmond kicked only four goals in the last quarter, Ronaldson and I each kicked two, which was lovely karma as we both had come up through the ranks of the under-19s at Tigerland together.

Here's an amazing fact about that Grand Final. The average number of games of the Richmond side that day was just 59, and no Grand Final winner since has had a lower player game average.

We were all a bunch of young kids, shepherded by just a handful of older players – Swift, Roger Dean, Paddy Guinane, Michael Patterson and Alan Richardson. As a result the 1967 premiership was the day the term 'Hafey's Heroes' was born and is still referenced to this day. We celebrated the premiership that night upstairs at McClure's restaurant in St Kilda.

Back row, from left: Kevin Sheedy, Kevin Shinners, Mick Erwin, Francis Bourke, Mike Bowden, Geoff Strang, Dick Clay, Royce Hart, Graham Burgin, John Perry. **Third row:** Neil Busse, Michael Green, Mike Perry, Neville Crowe, John Ronaldson, Mike Patterson, Ross Warner, Barry Richardson, Tony Jewell. **Second row:** Billy Barrot, Alan Richardson, Paddy Guinane, Ray Dunn (pres), Fred Swift (capt), Tommy Hafey (coach), Roger Dean, Graeme Richmond (sec). **Front row:** Frank Dimattina, John Northey, Kevin Bartlett, Bill Brown, David Jacks, Don Davenport, Graeme Bond.

1967 Grand Final
September 23, 1967, MCG

Richmond	4.3	9.10	12.15	**16.18 (114)**
Geelong	3.3	7.6	13.7	**15.15 (105)**

Best: Richmond – Barrot, Hart, Brown, A. Richardson, Dean, Bartlett.
Geelong – Goggin, Sharrock, Farmer, West, Polinelli, Newland.
Goals: Richmond – Ronaldson 3, Hart 3, Brown 3, Bartlett 3, Barrot, A. Richardson, B. Richardson, Guinane.
Geelong – Sharrock 4, Wade 4, Goggin 3, Andrews, Eales, Ryan, Hynes.
Umpire: P. Sheales. **Attendance:** 109,396

Richmond
B:	R. Dean	F. Swift (c)	T. Jewell
HB:	G. Burgin	M. Perry	G. Strang
C:	D. Clay	B. Barrot	F. Bourke
HF:	J. Northey	P. Guinane	B. Richardson
F:	J. Ronaldson	R. Hart	W. Brown
R:	M. Patterson	A. Richardson	K. Bartlett
Res:	M. Green	J. Perry	
Coach:	T. Hafey		

Geelong
B:	G. Ainsworth	R. West	G. Rosenow
HB:	T. Farman	P. Walker	D. Marshall
C:	K. Newland	W. Closter	T. Polinelli
HF:	J. Sharrock	G. Andrews	G. Eales
F:	C. Mitchell	D. Wade	G. Hynes
R:	G. Farmer (c)	W. Ryan	W. Goggin
Res:	R. Graham	J. Scarlett	
Coach:	P. Pianto		

FEATHERED FRIENDS:
The 1968 Galah squad, players from left.
BACK: Bryan Quirk (Carlton), Tassie Johnson (Melbourne), John Wynne (West Perth), Graham Farmer (West Perth), Gary Dempsey (Footscray), Peter Hudson (Hawthorn), Des Meagher (Hawthorn), Don McKenzie (Essendon), John Sharrock (Geelong).
SECOND BACK: Gary Fenton (Sandringham, VFA), Graeme Sheppard (Cooee, Tasmania), Daryl O'Brien (North Melbourne), Rob Farmer (Collingwood), John Dugdale (North Melbourne), David Dyson (West Perth), Mike O'Brien (Redan, Vic Country), Royce Hart (Richmond), Greg Tootell (Caulfield Grammarians, VAFA.)
SECOND FRONT: Brian Roet (Melbourne), Alex Jesaulenko (Carlton), Neil Kerley (Glenelg), Wayne Richardson (Collingwood), Murray Leeder (West Perth), Ron Barassi (Carlton), Geoff Slade (Frankston, VFA), Billy Walker (Swan Districts).
FRONT: Fred Bayes (Box Hill, VFA), John Birt (Essendon), David Thorpe (Footscray), Kevin Bartlett (Richmond), Trevor Collins (Camberwell, VFA), Syd Jackson (East Perth), Geoff Bryant (Box Hill, VFA), Roger Hoggett (Western Suburbs, NSW).

1968 Galahs World Tour

The Galahs World Tour in 1968 was the trip of a lifetime. I was 21. I'd never been out of Australia before. I'd barely been interstate before. Harry Beitzel invited me to represent Australia in Gaelic football games in Europe and America. I was rooming with legendary 'Polly' Farmer, who tried to convince me I could get $7000 a year if I left Richmond and went to Geelong! With the North Melbourne trio of Ron Joseph, Daryl O'Brien and John Dugdale, I flew from San Francisco to Las Vegas. We hired a Lincoln convertible and drove around to casinos and nightclubs. We didn't stay in a hotel; we just drove around and then 24 hours later we went back to the airport. A highlight was seeing Dean Martin at The Sands. I remember Ron Joseph writing down every song. He wanted a record of the night. For some reason we played a match in Bucharest, Romania between ourselves. No one spoke English to us. One day I tried to find a milk bar. I saw milk cans out of the front of a shop, so I went in. A fellow customer scared the living daylights out of me when he asked, 'Is Ted Whitten on your touring party?' I asked how he knew of Ted Whitten. He said he'd lived in St Albans but had to come home because of his family.

KB
PLAYING THE GAME

1969 GRAND FINAL

Tom Hafey broke his own rules when he brought in Percy Cerutty to speak before the finals. The result was magnificent.

1969 was an interesting year for the club because we just scraped into the finals, and there was a big power struggle taking place between president Ray Dunn and his secretary, Graeme Richmond. I've always assumed at one stage of their lives, they shared a close friendship. Caught in the middle of this was Tom Hafey, who was struggling to hold onto his job. There was a lot of chatter during that year that Tommy was going to get the sack.

During the year, Tommy's father passed away yet on the day of his father's funeral, the newspaper headline read 'Hafey for Sack', which further upset Tommy and the team on a very sad occasion.

ROYAL PRESENCE: Queen Elizabeth was at the 1969 flag unfurling.

HE'S DONE IT AGAIN!: Tom Hafey is chaired from the ground. At far left (with the camera) is Mike Perry, a photographer by profession, who missed the Tigers' finals campaign through suspension.

FINEST MOMENT: Roger Dean holds aloft the 1969 premiership cup while accepting the congratulations of John Nicholls.

Somehow, the side rallied for him and we had a very important match against Carlton in round 19 (there were 20 rounds that season) to ensure we made the finals – and we did, thanks to the performance of Bill Barrot, who was moved to full-forward while Eric Moore was moved to the centre. Barrot ended up kicking eight goals in a half, all on champion Carlton full-back Wes Lofts. As a result, we fell into the final four in fourth place on percentage.

Keep in mind, we had failed to make the finals the previous year, despite being reigning premiers. In 1969, Tom Hafey did something that he had never done before, and never did again.

He allowed someone from outside of the playing group to not only attend the pre-match address, but to then speak to the players. Until that time, only Tommy had ever addressed the side. Not even Graeme Richmond or Ray Dunn were ever allowed into that room before a match. None of the players knew what was going to happen; we all made our way into the room to prepare to hear Tommy's pre-match address. But as he turned to the door, and was about to speak, in walked Percy Cerutty, leading Australian athletics coach. Cerutty had called Tommy earlier in the year and was quite concerned after hearing about the difficult year he was having. Percy was a great admirer of Tommy and vice versa – they had

FROM FOURTH TO FIRST: The premiership medallion and WEG poster.

been pals for years. In fact, the whole Richmond team had been down to Percy's home and camp, called Cerus, a year or so earlier. So given the close association, Percy had called Tommy and asked if he could speak to the team.

Tommy had no idea what Percy was going to talk about. I assumed Percy was going to talk about the importance of the match ahead, but instead he spoke only about Tommy. The man. The coach. How we all respected him and how dedicated he was to the club and the players.

I know Tommy was absolutely shocked, because he really would never speak about himself.

We were so motivated after hearing that. We went out and defeated Geelong by 118 points in the semi-final and it was the start of a fantastic finals series for us. We beat Collingwood by 26 points in the preliminary Final before winning our second premiership in three years, defeating Carlton by 25 points in the Grand Final.

I remember Michael Green's great game in the ruck against John Nicholls, and we had Dick Clay on the wing carving up the Blues. Barry Richardson played full-back and held Alex Jesaulenko to one goal. One of the turning points of the game I clearly remember occurred just before the three-quarter time siren. The ball got kicked down to the forward line and Eric Moore was under a floater and just stood there and took the mark, and was absolutely poleaxed by Lofts. But Eric was so brave.

He knew what was going to happen, yet he stood his ground. He got up from the knock, went back and kicked the goal to give us the momentum into the last quarter.

We were four points behind at three-quarter time but came out in the last quarter and kicked 4.7 to their two points. I can always remember Tommy telling us after the game that in that last quarter, we had the most number of kicks in a quarter for the whole season. Carlton, by way of contrast had the least, so it was clear how dominant we were in that final quarter.

Back row, from left: Back row: Dick Clay, Tony Jewell, Brian Shinners, Des McKenzie, Royce Hart, Mike Bowden, Ray Ball, Eric Moore, Don Davenport. **Third row:** Ron Thomas, John Ferguson, Geoff Strang, Anthony Smith, Michael Green, John Ronaldson, Barry Richardson, Rex Hunt, Ian Owen, George McInnes, Mike Perry. **Second row:** Colin Beard, Graeme Burgin, Billy Barrot, Ray Dunn (pres), Roger Dean (capt), Tommy Hafey (coach), Mike Patterson, Alan Schwab (sec), Francis Bourke, Kevin Bartlett. **Front row:** Brenton Miels, Graeme Bond, Bill Brown, Kevin Smythe, Graham Robbins, Derek Peardon. **Absent:** John Northey, John Perry, Kevin Sheedy.

1969 Grand Final
September 27 1969, MCG

Richmond	2.2	6.5	8.6	**12.13 (85)**
Carlton	1.4	2.7	8.10	**8.12 (60)**

Best: Richmond – Green, Bartlett, Clay, Barrot, Northey, Dean. Carlton – Quirk, Crane, Silvagni, Lofts, Walls, Goold.
Goals: Richmond – Barrot 3, Moore 2, Northey 2, Bartlett, Bond, Dean, Hart, Ronaldson. Carlton – Jackson 2, Nicholls 2, Crosswell, Jesaulenko, Gallagher, Walls.
Umpire: J. Crouch. **Attendance:** 119,165

Richmond
B:	K. Sheedy	B. Richardson	C. Beard
HB:	G. Strang	G. Burgin	I. Owen
C:	D. Clay	W. Barrot	F. Bourke
HF:	J. Northey	R. Hart	R. Dean (c)
F:	J. Ronaldson	E. Moore	B. Brown
R:	M. Green	M. Bowden	K. Bartlett
Res:	R. Hunt	G. Bond	
Coach:	T. Hafey		

Carlton
B:	B. Gill	W. Lofts	V. Waite
HB:	P. Pinnell	J. Goold	K. Hall
C:	G. Crane	I. Robertson	B. Quirk
HF:	S. Jackson	R. Walls	B. Crosswell
F:	P. Jones	A. Jesaulenko	I. Nicoll
R:	J. Nicholls (c)	S. Silvagni	A. Gallagher
Res:	I. Collins	T. Hopkins	
Coach:	R. Barassi		

SHY COUPLE: Denise and I show off the 1967 premiership cup at the Tigers' 1968 family day.

KB
PLAYING THE GAME

MEETING DENISE

I met Denise during the 1967 preliminary final. She proved to be a tower of support during my entire footy career — and a strong critic every Saturday.

I first met my wife Denise at, where else, but the football. She was working at a drapery shop and got to know Bill Barrot, who was a sales rep who dropped into the shop from time to time.

He actually took her as his date to the 1967 preliminary final between Geelong and Carlton. The whole Richmond team went to watch the match, to get an insight into who we would be playing the next week and we all had to sit together as a team in alphabetical order.

This meant that Bill was next to me, but he allowed Denise to sit in between us. My story is that Billy concentrated on the game and I concentrated on Denise. Denise was fantastic when I was playing. A Carlton supporter before we met, she supported me enormously throughout my career. Right through my stints as a player, commentator and coach, she raised all four children and never complained about the long hours I was away from home because of my football commitments.

She was a football critic and knew a lot about the tactics of game, what I had to do to play well, and who may have let the club down when we lost. After games, she would tell me what went right, what didn't and why we won or lost. She was a great source of feedback and she didn't pull any punches.

During the 1973 season, Denise was pregnant with our first child. I played in the winning Grand Final and our first child Sharna, was born a few days later on October 4.

LOVE AND MARRIAGE: From above, the wedding day; a Tiger family; and during a post-season trip to Japan. The trip was a media award.

That night, everyone was down at the club for the premiership photo and I kept getting phone calls from the club to the hospital wanting to know if I was going to make it back for the photo shoot, because they were delaying it in the hope I would make it there in time. But Denise was still in labour and so I never got to the club in time.

That explains why, in the official 1973 team photo, I am featured as a little insert, on the right hand side of the photo.

KB
PLAYING THE GAME

A FEW CUPS WITH TOMMY

The coach put his faith in the players and the players gave everything for the coach. He had a common touch that brought uncommon results.

Len Smith stepped down as coach of Richmond in 1965 because of ill-health and the early talk was that Ron Branton, a former Richmond captain and three-time club best and fairest, was going to be his replacement. Branton was coach of Myrtleford at the time.

After some time, a chap named Tom Hafey entered the picture and I have to confess I'd never heard of him. He was coaching Shepparton. He got the job ahead of Branton. The first time I saw Tommy was at pre-season training in 1966. We were going to run the Tan Track, which would become a tradition under his coaching.

He turned up to this first training session in his running gear. He urged us to huddle around in a circle and then told us of his expectations of his first training run. All of a sudden he clapped his hand, said, 'Right, let's go,' and he led the pack off.

I still have this memory of Tommy running off into the distance to begin his lap of the Tan, leaving us all gobsmacked. It surprised most of us because Len Smith was an older gentleman who wasn't really into the personal fitness side of things. He and Tom Hafey were polar opposites in that respect.

Tommy did everything at full speed and ran himself absolutely ragged. My memory is that he was the first home around the Tan and he grabbed the attention of all players from that first training session. The following night we went over to a park where there was a 400-metre track and he made us run 10 400s. Sure enough it happened again! Tommy took part in the training, pumping his little legs through 10 400-metre repetitions. He wasn't super quick, but he ran himself to a standstill.

HEADY CLIMB: Hafey is lauded as a premiership maestro who draws from his country roots.

FLAG NUMBER FOUR: I celebrate the 1974 premiership, the fourth we won together, with the man who's had so much influence on me.

Even if he trailed the field he would keep on running. He had been playing in the country and he was as fit as most footballers at Tigerland.

"Enthusiasm is catching," he would always tell me. "So is the lack of it."

His attitude to fitness was an important reason why we became such a good side. Not only did we recruit well and develop good footballers, we were the fittest team. Tommy instilled into us that no team would be able to withstand Richmond pressure for 100 minutes; sooner or later they would crack.

He had a tremendous love of his players and the feeling was reciprocated. Thinking about it now, I believe a lot of us played for Tommy more so than the club, because as far as a lot of us were concerned Tom Hafey was the club.

When we lost, many players would feel as though they had let Tommy down. They were embarrassed to look him in the eye. That's the sign of a great coach. Tom never played favourites. He will never name a team of his best players. Everyone who played under him has a special place in his heart for Tommy. Every year at Christmas Tommy invites every player and official he coached or worked alongside to a function at a pub and he picks up the bill. Up to 70 turn up from all over the country.

Hafey's place at Richmond is assured for all time. He coached the club to four premierships – 1967, 1969, 1973 and 1974 – with the '67 triumph snapping a 24-year drought between Tiger premierships. His love of the game was contagious. He passed on his work ethic on to his players and he was ahead of his time by creating goals for each player. He was greatly loyal to his players and he held them in great trust.

Many think our game-plan under Tom was simply to get the ball and kick it long, but that's not right at all. The onus was on us to win any contest for the ball and then kick long to advantage. We were trained to run hard and get to the foot of every pack. It was all about helping out your teammate.

Tommy was always talking about games and showing images of game situations. He wanted to demonstrate that Richmond players should outnumber their opponents around the ball.

He had little black notebooks and he'd read stats from them during his pre-match address. These notes were a terrific source on the strengths and weaknesses of the opposition; they were crammed full of stats on marks, handballs, kicks and the capabilities of opposition players.

Once Tommy picked the side, he never lost confidence in the players. If we started slowly, he never panicked and made rash changes. He picked certain players for certain positions knowing they were strong enough to beat their opponent and he backed them to do so. He had selected roles for players based on his research and he wasn't going to change because they were struggling for a quarter or two. I think the players had enormous appreciation for his shows of faith. They knew that he had picked the best men for the job and that always lifted our spirits. Tommy always had a personal message for me when we spoke one-on-one before a match. He would ask how I was feeling, remind me of my importance to the side and of his confidence in me. His positive reinforcement was outstanding.

Off the field, Hafey wasn't so keen on players going to committeeman Ron Carson's garage after training, because they would pretty much spend the evening drinking. But he showed interest in all his players beyond footy. He wanted to know how they were doing at work or school and what was the latest with their families.

There was a tremendous bond between his players. Every 21st birthday, every engagement and every wedding was like a club function. Everyone went to them. There were no cliques in the club. Everyone was seen as an equal.

After many games we would go back to his place and everyone would be there. It was open house. He would bring in stacks of Kentucky Fried Chicken and drinks. It was as though Tigerland had been moved from Punt Road to Tom's house.

A QUIET WORD: Tom had a keen interest in every player and their views, and the players loved him for it. Note that the door at the back does not lead to secret meetings; it's the door of the secretary's office.

TOTAL TOM: Hafey (left) gets his message across while Bill Boromeo looks on; (from left) Neville Crowe, Mike Patterson, Hafey, Alan Richardson and Frank Dimattina at the Caulfield racecourse.

NEW GROUND: Tom (above) accepts the winner's trophy at the 1973 national championships; the clipping (left) describing Tom's exit from Punt Road; the clipping (far left) revealing Tom's Magpie shock.

He wanted to generate a family among the players and the club that would make it an irresistible force.

Before long, he became an important person in most of our lives. He was many players' longest-serving coach, so the bonds were really tight.

In 1968, a season after our drought-breaking premiership, we surprised everyone by missing out on the finals. In '69 we started slowly once again, leading to 'Hafey to be sacked' headlines. I couldn't believe what I was reading and nor could my teammates. He had become such an important part of our lives. Perhaps we were letting him down.

We ended up winning the premiership that year and I still firmly believe that the side lifted because of the talk about Tommy getting the sack. We scraped into fourth spot and then played an extraordinary final series. In the first final we defeated Geelong by 20 goals in a breathtaking performance. We defeated Collingwood in the preliminary final and we easily defeated Carlton in the Grand Final. In those days, winning a flag from fourth was considered almost impossible, but we did it with ease.

SUPER COACH: Tom addresses John Ronaldson (left), Graeme Bond and Michael Bowden; Tommy and I show off the cup from the Australian football championships in 1980. I was the Victorian captain and Tom was coach.

Tommy Hafey has been, apart from my parents, the greatest influence on my life. He gave me not only footy guidance but life skills. He was interested in me, and all his players, as a person, not just a footballer.

He inspired me to get better, to achieve. He treated me no different from any other player. He gave us everything so we could achieve greatness at Tigerland. Our friendship spans 45 years. We just clicked when we first met. He is godparent to my first daughter, Sharna, as is Maureen, who was great with all the wives and girlfriends. She brought them all together. Tom and Maureen were a great team.

For 10 years, Tommy and I met for lunch every Monday, Wednesday and Friday at the Commonwealth Café in Spring Street. Even when he coached Collingwood, he never missed our lunch engagement. I'll never forget the day he was sacked as coach of Collingwood in the middle of the 1982 season. Tommy strode into my workplace and I said, 'How's the day been, Tom?' He said, 'I've had better. I've just been sacked as Collingwood coach.' I was shocked. Tommy was shocked. He never saw it coming.

I suggested that we skip lunch for there must be other things to occupy his mind, but he said, 'Don't be silly.' So there we were, sitting in the Commonwealth Cafe, twelve floors up overlooking Melbourne, having a roast lunch – with the biggest footy story of the year about to break.

Tommy's strength of mind was incredible. His ability to accept disappointment and get on with his life was no more evident than on that day.

He was more loyal to Collingwood than they were to him. Richmond actually offered him the coaching job back at Tigerland the day after Collingwood lost the 1981 Grand Final, the fifth Grand Final under Tom's direction. He had a contract with the Pies and that, in his mind, could never be broken.

North Melbourne wanted him as coach. Chairman Bob Ansett was hot to trot. But Tommy stayed loyal to his verbal contract with Collingwood.

Brisbane wanted to sack Robert Walls during the 1995 season and install Tommy as coach. He refused, telling Brisbane officials it was a dud act to pull the rug on a coach mid-season.

A MAN NAMED RICHMOND

Players and staff feared Graeme Richmond because of his ruthlessness, but there was no doubt about his effectiveness. He was a big reason why the Tigers reached the top.

Graeme Richmond was the biggest powerbroker and most influential figure at Richmond during a time when the Tigers were full of colourful football identities. Just before I started playing in Richmond's under-19s, Graeme told me that the Tigers needed rovers and that if I could keep improving there was an opportunity for me.

Looking back now, I think he was giving me a bit of confidence and setting me a goal to achieve.

As the seasons went on Graeme went from coaching the juniors to club secretary, but he became far more than a normal club secretary. He was also head of recruiting, club motivator, coaching soundboard, at some stages he was also a selector.

He was a powerbroker who exerted great control. He was responsible for the appointment of Tom Hafey. His fingerprints were all over the 1967, '69, '73 and '74 premierships, and his role in 1980 was prominent as well.

Somewhere along the way, Graeme gave up the role of club secretary because he was going into the hotel business. Alan Schwab took over as secretary, but Graeme remained on the board, and became a vice-president. He always had some title or another, but no matter his title he was always the most powerful person at the club.

Graeme had a dynamic personality and was an outstanding orator. He was always in the rooms talking to the players about their performances and their goals. On many occasions he made the young players feel like they were vital cogs in the wheel, and how important it would be to the team if they played well.

You knew he was a hard marker so if he did give you a pat on the back then you'd regard it as getting a real tick. He cast a spell over many because of his passion and charisma. I even asked him to speak at my wedding and he did; that was the sort of standing you held him in.

On some occasions, Graeme would stand up on a wooden bench in the dressingrooms and deliver a rousing speech. You'd stop whatever you were doing and listen as he described how important it was for the club to be successful. Other times, he would trot out the speech about "It's time to pay back Collingwood/Carlton for all the times they've beaten us," or he'd evoke the names of Tiger greats like Jack

MAIN MAN: Graeme Richmond, clearly the most influential official at Richmond during my era, had vaulting ambition and a volcanic nature. Players and staff feared him. Put simply, he could end your career.

Dyer, Billy Wilson and Roy Wright. Players and staff feared Graeme because of his ruthlessness. He was the most powerful administrator at the club. Put simply, he could end your career or he could extend your career.

In my case, he was involved in the decision not to appoint me as captain at the start of 1976. In fact I was stripped of the vice-captaincy as well.

After winning the best-and-fairest in the premiership years of 1973 and '74, I had an ordinary year by my standards in '75. I was dumped as vice-captain but no reason was given.

I never complained nor asked for an explanation, but I do remember pausing before leaving the room and giving Graeme, president Ian Wilson, match committee chairman Allan Cooke and Tommy Hafey one last stare. I didn't speak and then I left. Later on, I remember that president Ian Wilson told me before I left the room that 'we want you to concentrate on playing footy.' But I felt betrayed by those who had pumped up my tyres for 10 years. I was devastated that they had lost confidence in me.

Looking back, being dumped as vice-captain matured me. I was no longer brainwashed by the Tigers. I became suspicious of what was said and done. Certainly, I became very wary of Graeme Richmond. You don't become the Godfather for no reason.

I became even more sensitive when Tommy rang me before the 1977 season to tell me he had quit as coach. He said he no longer had the support of Graeme. I knew Graeme wanted Tommy out. He had rung Tommy's brother Peter, who was the club runner, to ask him to convince Tommy to resign.

Tommy rightfully felt that it would be fruitless to continue as coach without Graeme's support. I remember saying to Tommy over the phone that the players love him and play for him. But Tommy's mind was made up. I became more wary of Graeme. How could the club's greatest ever coach not have the support of its most influential decision-maker? Tommy lived and breathed Richmond. Why did

SOLID WORK: Graeme Richmond plans further glory for the club (top) and taps a barrel with Francis Bourke at one of his pubs.

IT'S OURS... Kevin Bartlett, Royce Hart, Ian Wilson, Tom Hafey and Graeme Richmond with the premiership cup.

POWER AND PASSION: Richmond (above, far right) celebrates with coach and players.

Graeme turn on Tommy? I will never know. The dynamic between Graeme and I changed during my time as the Richmond coach. After I was sacked late in 1991, I was speaking to a well-respected journalist who was one of Graeme's close friends. The journalist told me out of the blue that, during my time as Tigers coach, Graeme had called a number of media friends to a lunch to put it on them to make life difficult for me. This journalist even went as far to say that Graeme deliberately sent people down to the dressing-rooms after a game to be abusive towards the players and me, in an effort to create unrest and dissatisfaction.

Next to Tommy, Graeme Richmond was the single biggest influence behind Richmond becoming a successful club. His recruiting, his passion, his drive and motivation talks remain legendary. Throughout the journey, I respected Graeme Richmond enormously. I'm just not sure, however, that I admired him.

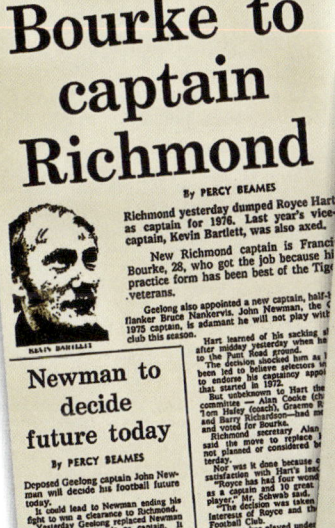

UPS AND DOWNS: The newspaper clippings depict Tom's exit before the 1977 season (right) and Bourke's elevation to the captaincy for the 1976 season.

KB

PLAYING THE GAME

'HUNGRY'

At Richmond I was KB or simply K. To television viewers, I was known by a famous reference to my love of a goal and my aversion to handball.

One nickname usually suffices for most sportsmen, but over my journey I ended up with two. If someone says 'Hungry' or 'KB', then they're referring to me. Lou Richards, who was responsible for so many wonderful nicknames in his newspaper column, was the creator of the 'Hungry' moniker.

It is a very clever nickname.

Lou, in cahoots with his ghostwriter Tom Prior, previewed that day's games in *The Sun* on Saturdays. Every week Lou sprinkled his columns with some of the great nicknames. The 'Galloping Gasometer' (North Melbourne ruckman Mick Nolan), the 'Flying Doormat' (Carlton defender Bruce Doull) and 'Lethal' (Hawthorn champion Leigh Matthews) were among his finest creations.

He called me Hungry for a couple of reasons. The first was that he decreed I never passed the ball, preferring instead to always have a shot at goal. The second was that I never handballed. To me, the nickname was a term of endearment.

Actually I wasn't even the first Hungry at Richmond. Billy Wilson, a rover through the 1940s and '50s, had that nickname. Billy would have played against Lou, who all those years later must have felt the Hungry tag was appropriate for me as well. When I first started out, I was known by my full name Kevin Bartlett. Then it became Kevin, then to just 'K', before my teammates finally settled on 'KB'. It may surprise people to know that Tommy Hafey never called me Hungry or KB, but rather 'K' or Kevin. The newspapers of the time were partly responsible for the KB moniker. It fitted succinctly into headlines, never failing to inform the reader of the subject of the story.

Only the fans and commentators called me Hungry, never my teammates or coaches. I quickly grew to love the nickname and even now in general conversation I play up to it. When people approach me on the street and talk about the fact that I never handballed, I tell them it's not true. I did handball – at training, twice, and both times to myself.

Some ask me why I didn't pass to Michael Roach if I was, say, 80 metres from goal. I always respond, that if I was that close to goal, I might as well have a shot. And if anyone brings up statistics that show I rarely tackled in a game, I've got a response for that, too. It's hard to tackle someone who had the ball so often.

UNMATCHED: I kicked 21 goals in the 1980 finals series. Here I celebrate one of eight against Geelong in the second semi-final at Waverley Park.

The Lace-up Guernsey

Lace-up guernseys were first spotted at Tigerland when Craig McKellar, a lanky ruckman from Woodville, came to Richmond in 1971. I remember when he ran out on to the training track wearing this green and gold lace-up top, which was made by a gentleman in South Australia called Vic Hill.

Immediately, a few of us liked the concept and the look of it, so we approached club secretary Alan Schwab, who organised to get some shipped over from Adelaide. Not everyone at Richmond wore them, but those of us who did loved them. The woollen jumpers of the time used to get so heavy on wet, muddy days. But the lace-up jumper was made out of canvas. It was close-fitting and when laced up really tight, it was hard to grab and didn't hold water. Plus, during a break in play, I would loop my mouthguard around the laces, rather than put it down my sock. I felt comfortable in it.

The only time I didn't wear a lace-up was during the odd game when the conditions were really appalling and I would don a long sleeve. My lace-up came with a leather lace, but occasionally I would lose it, so I used to get a very long shoelace and simply lace it up with that. The jumper I wore in my 403rd and last game of football has that shoelace as the lace. I wore lace-up jumpers from 1971 right up until 1983. They lasted another few seasons after that, but were banned when Melbourne champion Robert Flower badly hurt his finger by getting it caught in an opponent's lace-up jumper during a match. The League decided they were too dangerous. It was a ridiculous ruling and remains that way. Lace-up jumpers are a tradition of the game, going back to the early years of football. It would be fabulous to see them as part of modern football.

SAVOURED CUP: Richmond recruiter Roy Weston and I display our good fortune in 1973. It was a cup that was treasured after the letdown of 1972.

KB
PLAYING THE GAME

1973 GRAND FINAL

The loss to Carlton in the 1972 Grand Final sent the Tigers reeling. There was no way we were going to mess up during the rematch a year later.

After we won the 1969 premiership, we failed to make the Grand Final in the next two seasons. In 1972 we made it through to the premiership decider and were the warm favourites to defeat Carlton. Our final score that day of 22.18 (150) should have been good enough to win it. But sadly for us, the Blues kicked 28.9 (177) to win the highest-scoring Grand Final ever.

That loss in 1972 really knocked the stuffing out of Tom Hafey. We used to have lunch together three times a week, and after that Grand Final loss he was absolutely devastated and quite disillusioned.

He felt that to allow Carlton to kick the record score against us was humiliating. I personally reckon the Tom Hafey suffered from depression for up to three months after the 1972 Grand Final loss. He really felt the burden of that defeat, and his recovery took some time.

His depression drove him mad. In the end he willed himself to forget, to put it behind him.

Once he did, we were up and running once more and as fate would have it, the 1973 Grand Final offered our chance at redemption as we once again faced off against Carlton. The loss to Carlton the previous year had driven us all season and was still there when we met for breakfast on the morning of the Grand Final at Punt Road.

Once that had finished we were expecting Tommy to give his usual team meeting that took regularly place in the committee room and which

YELLOW AND BLACK: The '73 premiership pennant and WEG poster.

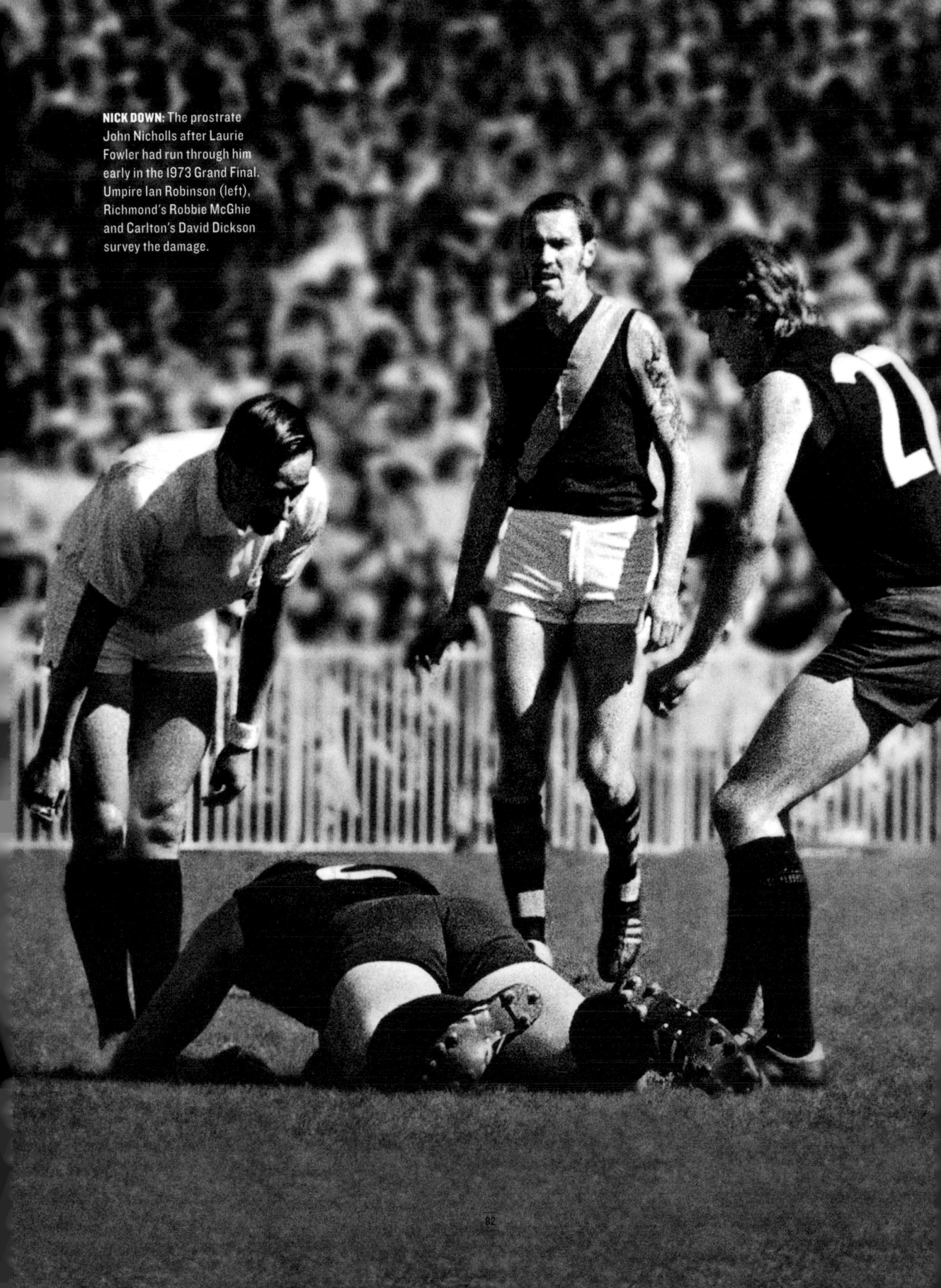

NICK DOWN: The prostrate John Nicholls after Laurie Fowler had run through him early in the 1973 Grand Final. Umpire Ian Robinson (left), Richmond's Robbie McGhie and Carlton's David Dickson survey the damage.

usually lasted for 40 minutes and sometimes longer. But this time he was about five minutes into the meeting and was literally in the middle of a sentence about a match-up when he stopped, looked at us and said, "There is nothing more to say, we are ready to go." And with that he ended the meeting. I think Tommy sensed that as a team, we were on a mission and were in the right frame of mind. And so we all walked across Yarra Park to the MCG as a really tight team, saying not a word.

It turned out that we won an extraordinary Grand Final. It started badly for Carlton when champion ruck-rover Barry Armstrong suffered from appendicitis in the week of the game and couldn't take his place in the side.

And then in the first few minutes our back-pocket Laurie Fowler knocked out John Nicholls, by jumping straight into him front on. He wouldn't get away with that type of action these days, but on this particular day, the psychological edge was all ours as the Blues came to terms with seeing their champion captain-coach rendered virtually ineffective.

And then Neil Balme added further fuel by violently attacking Geoff Southby and anyone else nearby in a navy blue jumper creating more mayhem. The other thing I remember distinctly was that Kevin Sheedy kicked three goals in the first quarter and played a fantastic game. It was a fabulous effort by 'Sheeds', who had been carved up in the back-pocket by Trevor Keogh 12 months before.

Like everyone at Richmond, he had a point to prove. I kicked a goal that day, but if you look at the scores and the stats, it was a team effort on the day. It was just a great day to be a part of Richmond.

YOU BEAUTY: The 1973 premiership medallion.

Back row, from left: Stephen Rae, Glynn Hewitt, Merv Keane, Bryan Wood, Eric Leech, Grant Allford, Francis Jackson, Dick Clay, Marty McMillan. **Third row:** Graeme Teasdale, Bill Nalder, Robert McGhie, Neil Balme, Craig McKellar, Brian Roberts, Michael Green, Barry Richardson, Rex Hunt. **Second row:** Kevin Morris, Roger Dean, Tommy Hafey (coach), Ian Stewart, Al Boord (pres), Royce Hart (capt), Alan Schwab (sec), Francis Bourke, Wayne Walsh, Kevin Sheedy. **Front row:** Robert Lamb, Paul Sproule, Daryl Cumming, Noel Carter, Laurie Fowler, Murray Thompson. **Absent:** Kevin Bartlett.

1973 Grand Final
September 29, 1973, MCG

Richmond	3.5	11.8	15.11	**16.20 (116)**
Carlton	2.2	7.6	9.9	**12.14 (86)**

Best: Richmond – Bartlett, Sheedy, Green, Stewart, Hart, Sproule.
Carlton – Crane, Walls, McKay, Hall, Pinnell, Jesaulenko.
Goals: Richmond – Hart 3, Sheedy 3, Stewart 3, Balme 2, Walsh, Roberts, Bartlett, Carter, Green.
Carlton – Crane 2, Dickson 2, Hall 2, McKay 2, Walls 2, Chandler, Nicholls.
Umpire: I. Robinson. **Attendance:** 116,956

Richmond
B:	L. Fowler	D. Clay	R. Hunt
HB:	M. Keane	F. Bourke	R. McGhie
C:	B. Wood	I. Stewart	W. Walsh
HF:	K. Sheedy	R. Hart (c)	S. Rae
F:	M. Green	N. Balme	N. Carter
R:	B. Roberts	P. Sproule	K. Bartlett
Res:	C. McKellar	K. Morris	
Coach:	T. Hafey		

Carlton
B:	R. Byrne	G. Southby	V. Waite
HB:	K. Hall	B. Doull	P. Pinnell
C:	D. Dickson	J. O'Connell	G. Crane
HF:	D. McKay	R. Walls	A. Jesaulenko
F:	J. Nicholls (c)	C. Davis	V. Catoggio
R:	P. Jones	B. Crosswell	B. Walsh
Res:	N. Chandler	B. Quirk	
Coach:	J. Nicholls		

IT'S OURS: Royce Hart makes his way back through the crowd to embark on the lap of honour. In those days, the captain accepted the premiership cup on a dais in the members' reserve and then took it back to his teammates.

KB
PLAYING THE GAME

THE WINDY HILL BRAWL

A few sharp words and it was on. Players and officials rushed in from everywhere. I, meanwhile, was in the rooms drinking cordial.

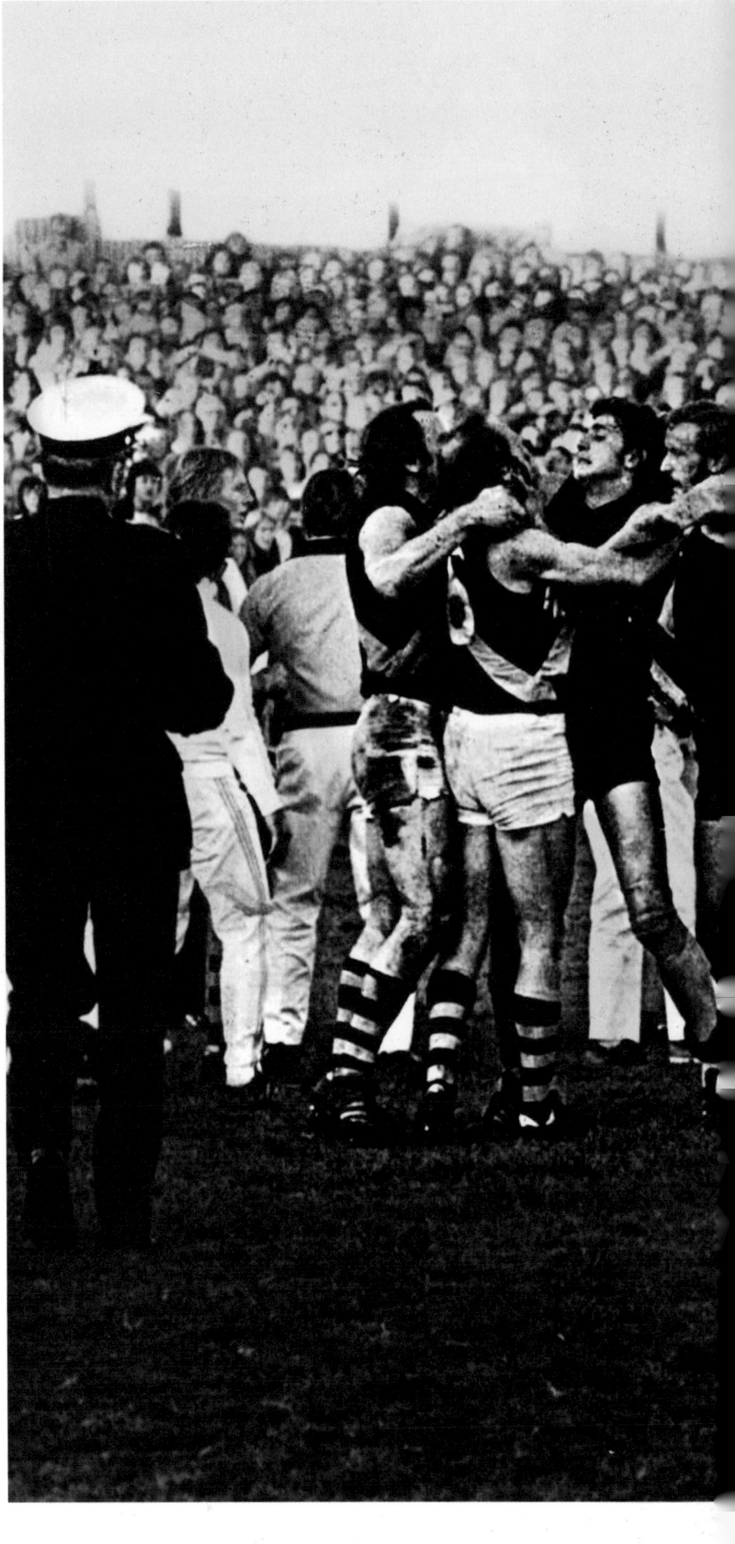

The Windy Hill brawl happened in round seven, 1974. I was filling in as Richmond captain. Regular captain Royce Hart had knee problems throughout the 1973 and '74 seasons and so he was not playing. Royce, however, drove Mal Brown to the game and claims that Mal turned to him in the car and said, 'Where is a good place at Windy Hill to start a fight?'

Just before half-time, Brown was coming off the ground, maybe because of an injury, and he had words with Laurie Ashley, who was Essendon's runner. The two men started an exchange just as the siren sounded. Graeme 'Jerker' Jenkin

PANDEMONIUM: Players, officials, police and a young supporter called James Ferguson (No.13) converge amid the mayhem of the 1974 brawl. Others include (from left) Bryan Wood (partially obscured behind trainer), Ian Stewart with his arm around Paul Sproule (No.6), and Essendon players Ken Roberts and Ken Fletcher. The Richmond player farthest away in the centre of the photo is Wayne Walsh. Next to him, Richmond committeeman Neil Busse is restraining Graeme Richmond while Robbie McGhie looks towards Essendon medico Dr Bill Grainger (with his back to the camera). Richmond half-back Merv Keane's head can be seen just over the policeman's shoulder; Mike Green's head is above his. Essendon wingman Gary Parkes has his head bowed.

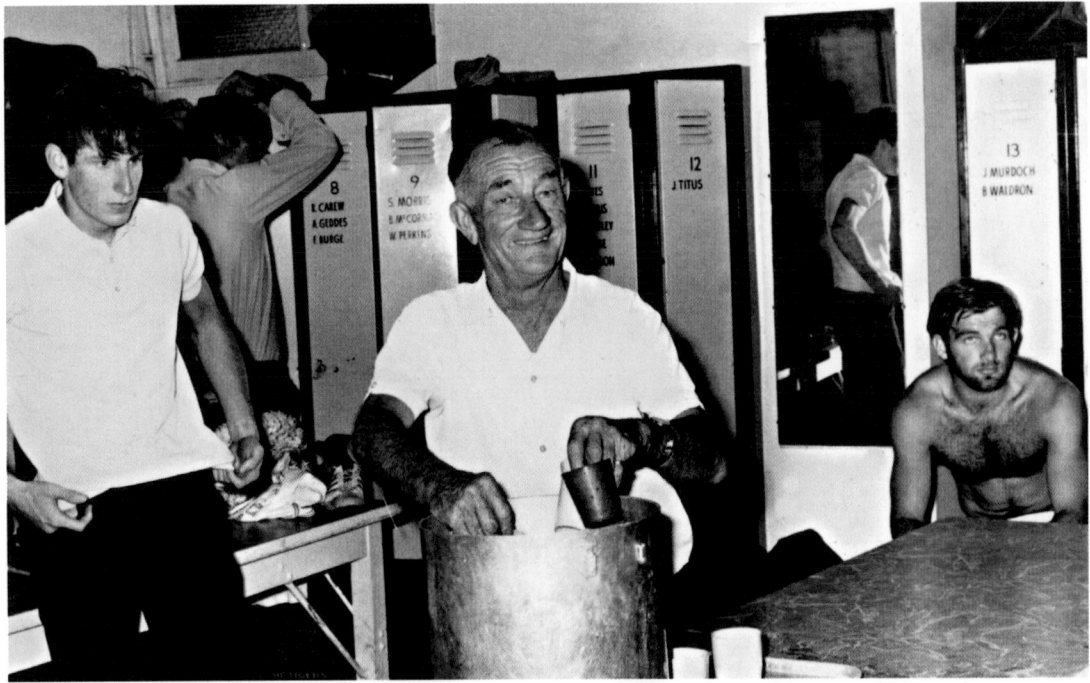

KING OF THE TRAINERS: Charlie Callendar (centre) was inside the rooms making cordial when the brawl broke out. At right is Michael Bowden, the father of the Bowden boys, Sean, Joel and Patrick, who played for Richmond in the 1990s and 2000s.

came across to get involved. I like to say that Mal grabbed Jerker's nuts and had a firm grip while he was yelling abuse at Laurie Ashley.

Essendon's Johnny Cassin launched himself from the bench into the confrontation, so Brown took him on, too, all the while holding firmly on to Jerker's nuts. Brown later recalled at the tribunal that Cassin was 'like Batman' flying in from the bench. The four of them, Mal and the three Essendon blokes, started a heated brawl and both teams came in to break that up.

Peter Hafey, the Richmond runner, once pointed out an interesting thing. Back then, the race for the visitors' rooms at Windy Hill was next to the Essendon coaching bench.

For the Tigers to get off the ground, we had to walk straight past the Essendon bench, and that caused further explosions. Richmond's Brian 'Whale' Roberts came in to defend his teammates and, as far I can recall, he sort of slipped and ended up being the perfect height for Essendon's Ron Andrews to go whack! Ronnie busted open the Whale's nose.

Graeme Richmond was sitting on the bench next to the runner (which is what he always did) and he flew off the bench into the melee. Essendon's fitness adviser Jim Bradley ran onto the ground and he and Graeme had a go at each other.

Richmond's Stephen Parsons, a 17-year-old in just his third senior game, saw out of the corner of his eye a man in a nondescript tracksuit attacking Graeme Richmond. Parsons thought it was a spectator on the ground so he ran up to him and floored him with a right. Turns out he had hit Jim Bradley.

While all this was going on, I had made it up to the players' race and was watching from there. I often say that I had to go into the Richmond rooms because our trainer, Charlie Callander, had spent so much time laying out the cordial and oranges that it would have been wrong for me to leave them to waste.

THE WASH-UP: The Windy Hill brawl created excitement for weeks afterwards, as shown by these headlines.

Parsons once said that going up the race was as scary as staying out on the ground. The race only went up to your hip so it was open slather for supporters.

One Bombers supporter was spitting on the Richmond players so Kevin Morris grabbed him by the collar and held him there as Robbie McGhie punched him in the head.

There was tremendous anger in the rooms at half-time – a really agitated buzz. Tommy was trying to settle down the players and get their minds back on the game.

Roberts didn't come back on after the break because of his broken nose and cut eye. Stephen Rae replaced him.

Parsons remembers sitting in the rooms at half-time and looking out to the glass walls. He says the glass was pulsating from the rage that was on the Essendon side. In the end, we got up by 10 points.

A lot of people went to the tribunal. The Whale gave evidence that he thought he'd been kicked by a policeman's horse, which was a farcical comment but typical comment of those days. Graeme Richmond was fined and it took a long time for the club to pay it. President Ian Wilson was in Spain on the day of the brawl. Eventually he returned and paid the fine. When Graeme Richmond found out he approached Wilson and said, 'You weak bastard!'

The Windy Hill brawl galvanised the Tigers players, who developed a great sense that 'the world was against Richmond'. Just about everyone at our club seemed to have been fined or suspended. We used that attitude as motivation to win the premiership that year.

MISSED BY THAT MUCH: I strain (left) to hear the 1974 Brownlow Medal count, with Denise at my side.

KB
PLAYING THE GAME

THE ELUSIVE BROWNLOW

What does a man have to do? I was favoured to win football's highest honour on several occasions but I always fell short.

I had plenty of terrific seasons that suggested I was a chance for the Brownlow, but of course I never won. Footy history is littered with instances in which fancied players have failed to win in a medal. I'm just one of many.

There were four times when I was a leading contender. In 1968 I shared the favouritism with Bob Skilton. I was the outright favourite in 1974 and I was highly regarded in 1977 and again in '78.

In 1968, I won Richmond's best and fairest and six media awards. My prizes included a new Holden car from Dustings, valued at $2512, and a trip for two to Japan from Malaysia-Singapore airlines, valued at $2613. Yet in the Brownlow I polled just 10 votes – three best-on-grounds and a one vote – and finished in 17th place, 14 votes behind Skilton.

I ended up taking the trip to Japan with my fianceé Denise (who I later married). Not one person we met on the trip spoke English, let alone had heard of Australian Football.

We were gone for 10 days, and mostly we just wandered around. The locals often stopped Denise because she had blonde hair. We went up to the top of Tokyo Tower, up the cable cars to Mt Victoria, and we witnessed a traditional tea ceremony.

You wouldn't believe it; at the tea ceremony, they had to choose someone from the crowd to be the guest of honour and drink the tea – and they chose me. Now I love my tea, but I refused to take the stage to drink Japanese tea. I just shook my head, waved my hand and politely declined.

NEAR AND FAR: An *Inside Football* headline predicting my victory and (below) some Richmond's best-and-fairest awards and a medal for a VFL team-of-the-year award.

SWAN SONG: I shared favouritism with Bob Skilton before the 1968 Brownlow count, but he scored 24 votes to win his third medal, while I finished well back on 10 votes.

There's no doubt that winning a Brownlow would be a wonderful achievement, especially given the award's historical significance. But I always believed that winning a premiership was the most important honour in football. At the start of every season, the flag was my sole motivation.

Twice I could have won the Brownlow on the last vote of the night and, yes, there was a fleeting sense of disappointment. But I always took a philosophical approach: a lot of things went my way and I enjoyed plenty of success during my journey through football.

Perhaps if I'd played in a side that was less successful the Brownlow might have had more significance, but failing to win never affected me in any way, shape or form.

I always kept in mind the fact that the Brownlow was decided by votes given by the umpires straight after every match. The votes were cast well before the medal count, so you'd either won or you hadn't. The speculation and the betting were irrelevant; there was nothing you could do on the night to change anything. I was quite indifferent to it all.

I have always believed that the Brownlow Medal must remain an award decided by the umpires. I will never waver from that opinion. The umpires are the most unbiased people in footy. They have no official association with clubs and are rarely former players. All Brownlow winners have stood the test of time and, certainly, no one has won the Brownlow Medal after a poor season.

The AFL Players' Association awards have grown in importance over the years. Some fine awards have been introduced, like the Madden Medal and Most Courageous Player award. But I firmly believe, irrespective of the growing prestige of the AFL MVP award, it will never challenge the Brownlow Medal. There are large books written about Brownlow winners, not so for the MVP.

I understand people becoming concerned that the Brownlow has become an on-ballers' medal, but then they are in the play more and have more opportunities to be noticed. Let's face it, clubs also put great priority in a deep midfield.

Every club has up to 10 players rotating through their midfield. If you multiply that by 17 clubs, that makes 170 players who are regularly in the umpires' gaze. On the other hand, there's only a handful of key-position players and they're barely rotated. So the odds are strong that a midfielder will win it and for me that's not a concern at all.

In 1974 I won every media award except for one. But of more importance to me was the fact that the Tigers were in contention for back-to-back premierships. That was my driving ambition

ROO BOY: Keith Greig (left) won the 1973 Brownlow with 27 votes. I was no pal of the umpires that year, polling just eight votes.

towards the end of the season, not the prospect of winning the Brownlow.

Well before the Brownlow became a glamorous affair, we had the *Truth* newspaper's Cazaly Awards, named after South Melbourne and St Kilda legend Roy Cazaly. The main award was the forerunner to what we now call the most valuable player award. The voting was revealed in the paper every week before going 'in camera' after round 16 in order to enable the suspense to build on the awards night.

And what nights they were. They would award Silver Cazalys for the best player in each position, before announcing the winner of the Gold Cazaly for the best player in the league, which was presented by Mrs Roy Cazaly.

In 1973 and '74 I won back-to-back Gold Cazalys. But in the 1973 Brownlow, I polled just eight votes and finished 19 votes behind the winner, North Melbourne's Keith Greig. Twelve months later I was the clear favourite to win the Brownlow. On the morning of count, four writers from *The Age* – Percy Beames, Ron Carter, Paul Speelman and Mike Sheahan – all tipped me to win.

In those days, before the votes were read out on a game-by-game basis, the VFL used to like stringing out the excitement to the very end. The one votes were read first, followed by the twos and then the threes. League executive director Eric McCutchan kept the suspense going all night and when it came to the crunch he said, 'And the final vote, ladies and gentleman is K…' and then he paused for what seemed a very long time. It could only be 'K. Greig', or 'K. Bartlett.'

I remember that the then *The Sporting Globe's* chief football writer, Greg Hobbs, was sitting at my table in 1974. As McCutchan paused, Hobbs pulled some money out of his wallet, dramatically threw it

SO CLOSE: I was marked in as the Brownlow favourite again in 1974 but again Keith Greig won, while I picked up Truth's Cazaly award and the Winfield Medal for the best player in the interstate carnival. At least I polled better in the Brownlow than other years. Keith scored 27 votes, Melbourne's Gary Hardeman scored 23 while I finished third on 22.

on the table and yelled across to me, 'You'll win the Brownlow on the last vote of the night!'

McCutchan finished his sentence with the name 'Greig'. So Keith Greig won with 27 votes, Melbourne's Gary Hardeman finished second with 23 votes, and I was third on 22 votes (five best on grounds, three two votes and one single vote). I simply accepted the fact that I had lost. There was no animosity from me whatsoever. Keith Greig was a fantastic player in 1974, but Richmond was a top club and perhaps there was a bit of arrogance about us. Some of those at Richmond were incensed by the result.

Alan Schwab and Ian Wilson had a slanging match with North Melbourne officials later that night, saying that, while Greig had had a fine season, I deserved the Brownlow. Naturally, those remarks made it into the press the following day and the media had a field day reporting on this 'feud' between the Tigers and the Kangaroos.

Don't forget, Richmond and North Melbourne were the two main contenders for the premiership that year, so there was already plenty of tension between the two clubs.

North was the up-and-coming club. Ron Barassi had put together a very good side, aided by the short-lived 10-year rule, which brought the stars Barry Davis (Essendon), Doug Wade (Geelong) and John Rantall (South Melbourne) to Arden Street. North's recruiting bonanza was controversial.

With this in mind, perhaps Schwab and Wilson were incensed that one of their players had 'lost' the Brownlow.

It was certainly bad sportsmanship and it cast the club in a bad light. Richmond players weren't arrogant at all. We just did our best for Tom Hafey. The officials were responsible for Richmond's arrogant reputation.

I was a strident advocate for changing the Brownlow. When I retired at the end of 1983, I wrote a letter to League general manager Jack Hamilton urging the League to eliminate countbacks and to bestow retrospective awards.

I felt it was unfair that a player could score the same tally of votes as the winner and lose the Brownlow Medal on a countback.

My thinking was that if you got the same number of votes, you deserved to win. Players who had lost on countbacks often had voted in more games, meaning they had enjoyed a more consistent season than the player who had polled more best on grounds.

I believed that Verdun Howell, Noel Teasdale, Bill Hutchison, Col Austen, Harry Collier and Allan Hopkins all deserved to be recognised as Brownlow medallists. I used the analogy of a horse race. If there is a dead-heat, they don't award the race to the horse carrying the heavier weight.

And so, in 1989 a special retrospective Brownlow Medal night was held on which the League bestowed medals to those players or to family members of those no longer with us.

And that made me very proud.

MISSED AGAIN: Malcolm Blight (top, with League president Allen Aylett) won the 1978 Brownlow with 22 votes. I finished fourth with 19. In 1977 I finished second; Graham Teasdale scored 59 votes and I had 44. But I did win a Caltex Sports Star award and, as shown in this clipping, I had a good idea about retrospective awards for those who had lost on a countback. Such awards were made in 1989. I finished my career with 160 Brownlow votes, now in 13th place behind Gary Dempsey (246).

KEVIN'S MEDAL PLEA

By MIKE SHEAHAN

Kevin Bartlett, who has a chance tonight to become the oldest Brownlow Medal winner ever, has gone to bat for the joint winners who never got a medal.

Richmond's champion half-forward told today how he had been trying for nearly 18 months to get the VFL to provide a medal each for Herbie Matthews and Des Fothergill, who tied in the 1940 count.

Bartlett has always believed the pair deserved a medal each, but the league kept the medal and it stays at VFL House.

"Ever since I was a kid listening to Brownlow counts, I've always thought it was wrong that they tied with a record score and the medal was kept by the VFL," he said.

Bartlett, who has finished second, third and fourth in the medal, said it was "a shame" for Matthews and Fothergill that they did not possess football's most traditional award. He wrote to VFL general manager Jack Hamilton on the subject.

BEAUTIFUL DAY: Royce Hart leads his Tiger teammates in celebration after the 1974 Grand Final: (from left) Francis Bourke, Kevin Sheedy, Neil Balme and Merv Keane. Closer to the podium are me, Daryl Cumming, Barry Richardson (arms aloft), Brian Roberts, Robbie McGhie, Bryan Wood, Sir Henry Winneke (on podium), Sir Maurice Nathan, Hart and Mike Green.

KB
PLAYING THE GAME

1974 GRAND FINAL

Tom Hafey encouraged us to shake our opponents' hands before the game to show we weren't arrogant. Then we got the jump.

After our win in 1973, Tom Hafey laid out his plan to for us to achieve the really difficult goal of back-to-back premierships. No club had done so since Melbourne in 1959–60, but we were of a mind that 14 years had been long enough and the time had come for a club to achieve true greatness by winning consecutive premierships.

It was our third successive Grand Final appearance and the ultimate challenge for the club. But we were in the midst of Richmond's greatest era and one flag from three attempts would not be good enough.

I think the football public and even the media were hoping that

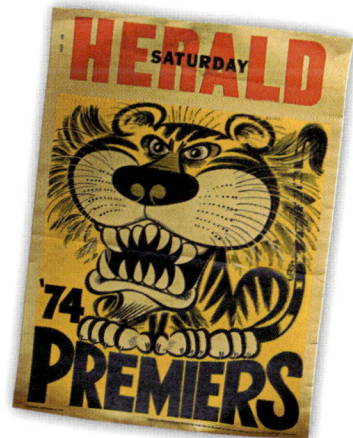

Back row, from left: Michael Green, David Cloke, Robert McGhie, Brian Roberts, Neil Balme, Gareth Andrews, Barry Richardson. **Middle row:** Dick Clay, Francis Bourke, Royce Hart, Tommy Hafey (coach), Kevin Bartlett, Paul Sproule, Kevin Morris. **Front row:** Kevin Sheedy, Merv Keane, Cameron Clayton, Daryl Cumming, Bryan Wood, Wayne Walsh. **Inset:** David Thorpe.

1974 Grand Final
September 28, 1974, MCG

Richmond	3.8	10.11	12.17	**18.20 (128)**
North Melb	3.2	8.3	11.4	**13.9 (87)**

Best: Richmond – Sheedy, Hart, Sproule, Green, Balme, Walsh.
North Melbourne – Greig, Cable, Schimmelbusch, Rantall, Smith, Burns.
Goals: Richmond – B. Richardson 5, Hart 3, Balme 2, Green 2, Sheedy 2, Cloke, Cumming, Thorpe, Walsh.
North Melbourne – Wade 4, Cable 2, Kekovich 2, Briedis, Burns, Davis, Greig, Peterson.
Umpire: I. Robinson. **Attendance:** 113,839

Richmond
B:	M. Keane	D. Clay	G. Andrews
HB:	F. Bourke	R. McGhie	K. Morris
C:	W. Walsh	D. Thorpe	B. Wood
HF:	D. Cloke	R. Hart (c)	P. Sproule
F:	N. Balme	B. Richardson	D. Cumming
R:	M. Green	K. Sheedy	K. Bartlett
Res:	B. Roberts	C. Clayton	**Coach:** T. Hafey

North Melbourne
B:	D. Pagan	D. Dench	B. Smith
HB:	J. Rantall	G. Farrant	K. Montgomery
C:	K. Greig	J. Burns	W. Schimmelbusch
HF:	S. Kekovich	P. Baker	P. Feltham
F:	P. Ryan	D. Wade	R. Peterson
R:	B. Goodingham	B. Davis (c)	B. Cable
Res:	G. Cowton	A. Briedis	**Coach:** R. Barassi

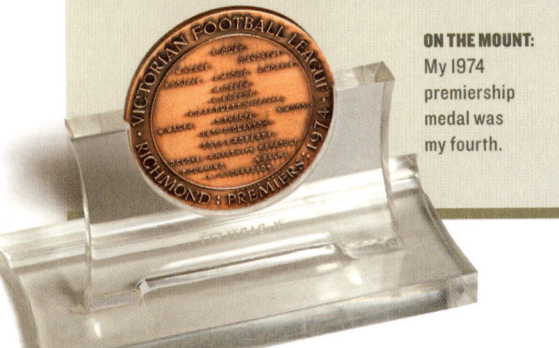

ON THE MOUNT: My 1974 premiership medal was my fourth.

North Melbourne, which had never won a premiership, could upstage Richmond and our perceived arrogance.

Tommy was very much aware of the bad feeling towards the club and I know he asked several of us before the game to make a point of seeking out Keith Greig during the pre-match warm-up and to shake his hand and congratulate him on winning the Brownlow. He hoped that small gesture would be picked up by the crowd and that they would realise that if there was any arrogance at Richmond it wasn't coming from the players.

Once the game got underway we jumped to the lead from the start and were never really challenged by North at any stage.

I remember well Kevin Sheedy's presence of mind to handball over the man on the mark to Michael Green in the goal square, it was the epitome of his cunning and an early sign of the 'outside the square' thinking that marked his brilliant coaching career with Essendon and his 'second career' as the AFL's big ideas man.

And I also remember Cameron Clayton, playing just his eighth senior game becoming the youngest ever Richmond premiership player. He had only turned 17 at the start of the season.

The team that played in the 1974 Grand Final was quite different to the team that won the flag in 1973.

Gareth Andrews had played for Geelong against us in the 1967 Grand Final. He joined us mid-season in a swap for Rex Hunt that surprised many around the club. Andrews ended up playing an important part in our powerful defence. He was a tremendous mark. He had an ungainly kicking style, but he was as brave as they come.

Another addition to our side was two-time Footscray best-and-fairest winner David Thorpe. David was a ball-winning machine who had caught the eye of Tom Hafey by always playing well against Richmond.

Although not a penetrating kick, he was a champion centreman and a reliable replacement

OUT TO MEET IT: Richmond defender Gareth Andrews tries to reel in the ball while I prepare to swoop on any crumbs. The other Richmond player (No.38) is half-back Kevin Morris. The North Melbourne players are (from left) Barry Cable, Phil Baker, Rob Peterson and Sam Kekovich.

for Ian Stewart, whose injuries had set him back. We also added a young kid by the name of David Cloke, who, at 19, was the second youngest member of the team. (Cameron Clayton, the 17-year-old 19th man, was the youngest.) In 1974 'Clokey' was tall and gangly and he played as a half-forward flanker. He contributed one goal in the Grand Final.

Barry Richardson came back into the side after missing the 1973 premiership with another knee injury. We played him at full-forward in 1974 and he kicked 5.1 in the Grand Final. It was the most incredible comeback.

Daryl Cumming, quick and creative with his handball, came into the premiership side having played in the losing Grand Final side in 1972. He kicked a goal.

Besides those changes, we were motivated by the fact that no team had won back-to-back premierships for a long time. It made us unstoppable.

TWO TRUE: A clipping heralding our successive premierships.

KB
PLAYING THE GAME

THE YEAR I QUIT THE TIGERS

First they overlooked me as captain. Then they stuck me out in starvation corner. Tommy was no longer at the club. It seemed right to go.

The culmination of a series of events over a few years nearly led to by departure from Richmond in 1979. I was deputy vice-captain in 1971 and vice-captain from 1972 to '74, a period when Roger Dean and then Royce Hart were captain. However during the 1973 and 1974 premiership seasons, with Royce suffering from a series of knee injuries, I captained the club on several occasions, including the infamous Windy Hill brawl match and at the end of both those seasons, I won the best and fairest. At the start of every season I set out with the goals of helping the team win each week, helping the team win a premiership and to play as well as I possibly could. In both 1973 and 1974, I could say that I achieved all three.

In 1975 we got to a preliminary final but lost to North Melbourne by 17 points at Waverley Park. By this time, the club had decided that Royce's time as skipper was up. I assumed I was next in line to be captain of the Richmond Football Club.

I was so close to the captaincy in 1976 that I could touch it. I was even named acting captain of the club in the lead-up to the start of the 1976 season, leading the team through all the practice matches, and I turned up to the club's family day just days before the start of the season expecting to be given the position on a permanent basis. But to my surprise and extreme disappointment, I wasn't even named vice-captain. Francis Bourke was named as captain and Neil Balme named as vice-captain. I held nothing against them as they were two of my favourite players and two of my closest friends, who I admire to this very day.

I had no inkling that I had missed out on the captaincy until I was called into the rooms at Punt Road at the family day. Allan Cooke, the chairman

SHOCK HEADLINE: My displeasure with the Tigers became public.

MAGPIE DREAMING: This photo was taken on the eve of the 1980 finals series. It was also the closest I got to becoming a Magpie.

of selectors, wandered out while I was busy signing some autographs out on the ground and asked me to come inside to the secretary's office for a chat. I expected at the time that he was going to outline the plans to announce me as captain. But I was wrong. There was no reason given whatsoever, except I remember president Ian Wilson later giving the age-old line about wanting me to concentrate on playing.

At the end of that year a lot of people believed Tom Hafey was sacked as coach of Richmond, but he actually resigned. He was supposed to coach the Tigers again in 1977, but he quit less than two weeks after being reappointed because he believed he didn't have the support of Graeme Richmond.

So Barry Richardson was appointed coach and he and Neil Busse, who was on the club's executive, asked if I would accept the vice-captaincy if it was offered to me. I said I would, although I'm sure that given what took place the year before, they might have been expecting me to tell them to 'go jump!'

But it was Barry's first year as coach and I wanted to support him as much as I could because he had big shoes to fill. In 1977 I won the best and fairest for the fifth and final time. By doing so, I equalled the record of the great Jack Dyer. And I also finished runner-up in the Brownlow Medal to South Melbourne's Graham Teasdale, a former teammate at Richmond. We finished fourth that year, losing to North Melbourne in the first semi-final at Waverley.

The next year I came second in the best and fairest and finished fourth in the Brownlow, just three votes behind North Melbourne's Malcolm Blight. The team finished seventh and missed the finals, which resulted in Barry Richardson getting sacked and Tony Jewell taking over. I was appointed captain in 1979 and all should have been well.

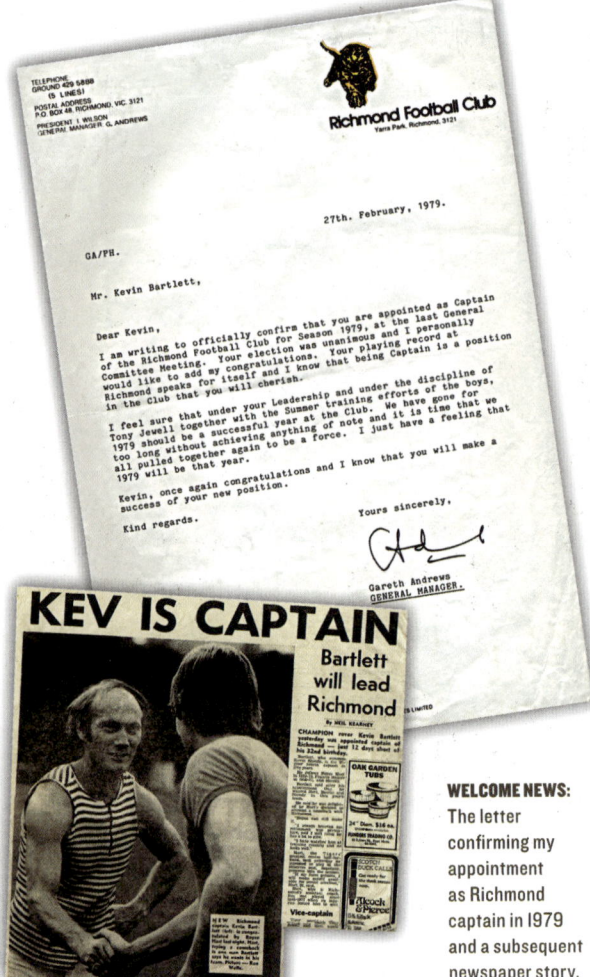

WELCOME NEWS: The letter confirming my appointment as Richmond captain in 1979 and a subsequent newspaper story.

Yet the gloss was taken off the appointment during the season when I discovered that, after 14 years, I was no longer in favour to be chosen as the rover. By the middle of the season, when I picked up the newspaper I was seeing my name listed on the half-forward flank. And there was no subterfuge back in 1979; the way the teams were picked in the paper was the way they lined up on game day.

There was nothing I could do to change it; the decision had been cast in stone. In those days, the half-forward flank was called the football graveyard, which meant you stayed out there. It was a position for opportunists and the play would sometimes take place everywhere but where you were placed on the field.

It all happened around the midway mark of the 1979 season. It was probably Graeme Richmond's idea, although he wasn't the one to break the news.

That task fell to Allan Cooke, who met me after training one night in the medical room. It was a deep discussion about the club as a whole and where the side was going, and I remember that by the end of this meeting I still had no idea what it was all about. Not once as we chatted did he ever make it clear that I wasn't roving, or that I was too old (I was then 32), or that it was time to go. Ian Wilson, the president at the time, still jokes about it. He tells me that someone had made a decision at the club that I was no longer going to be roving, but that nobody put their hand up, 'to be the one who tells KB.'

I think it fell to Cooke, but he didn't quite go through with it, so it wasn't until I was named as half-forward flank in the paper for the round 11 clash against Essendon at Waverley that I discovered I was no longer roving for the Richmond Football Club.

Back then, the biggest sports journalist in Melbourne was Rob Astbury. He was a TV reporter and was the news breaker in football. And as I walking to that game through the carpark, he was walking near me and he turned and said to me, 'I'm told that this is your last game for the Richmond Football Club.'

I was staggered because no one had ever said that, and here I was, the captain of the club. I had no doubt that Rob would not have said anything like that without good sources to back it up.

So I found myself taking those comments into the game and they certainly helped motivate me to play well. I kicked four goals that afternoon and was named in the best players. And to this day I am pretty certain if I had played poorly against the Bombers that day, then I more than likely would have been told that my career was finished.

I believe the club had made up its mind and had decided I was finished as a footballer. Kevin Sheedy had already retired that season and there were those who felt I should have been next.

Their plan was to leave me on the half-forward flank, let me become disillusioned, not get a kick, and then say goodbye to me. This is why I always hold a special place for Waverley Park, because it actually saved my career. I played the rest of the season at

KEVIN BARTLETT — Tigers' captain

half-forward with reasonable success, but after the last game, I decided to resign as captain because I genuinely felt that the club had lost confidence in me as a player. The club had tried to create a set of circumstances that would lead to me not playing well and leave me no alternative but to retire.

I informed the club of my decision shortly after the end of the season. I remember walking into the club and saying, 'I am resigning as captain of the club and as a player of the Richmond Football Club because I believe there are people at this club who are conspiring against me and therefore, to halt any of the problem whatsoever, I will resign, move on and play elsewhere because I feel I can play for another three years.'

We continued to have a number of meetings over the next week or so, at which I represented myself, and I just kept saying, 'I don't believe you want me to play and I can accept that. I can accept if you think I am finished and that I'm no longer the player you expect me to be. I am happy to take that heartburn off you and I will go and play elsewhere.'

I think that approach surprised them, because I don't think they anticipated that sort of thinking and I don't think they wanted me to move to another club. It wouldn't have been a good look for Richmond to have the club's games record holder, a four-time premiership player and five-time best and fairest suddenly bobbing up to play for another club. I suspect that it was at those meetings that they realised that they would have blood on their hands.

There was a bit of a media campaign against me as well. It's funny. I had noticed in the weeks leading up to being moved to the half-forward flank that there were some small articles in the paper that were critical of me, and I had come to understand the machinations of the footy club, that leaks can be deliberate and targeted and I was left in no doubt that those stories were being planted by the club to lessen the impact of pushing me to retirement.

When I had those few meetings with the club I kept telling them that I didn't believe that they wanted me to stay and that the leaks to the media were part and parcel of that. I kept repeating that I was happy to do their bidding in that respect. They asked me who I felt was responsible for the articles in the paper and I said, 'the people in this room', which were Ian Wilson and Graeme Richmond. But deep down I felt it was really Graeme's doing, although until the day he died, Graeme and I never re-visited the events of this period.

I always had a good relationship with Ian. He was the flamboyant president, wore his heart on his sleeve and brought a lot of arrogance to the club. But I didn't see Ian as a powerbroker, but more of a figurehead and a person very devoted to the club and keen to see it do well. But in terms of the playing side of things and the wheeling and dealing between clubs, I didn't believe that was Ian's domain. That was Graeme's self-appointed role.

During this time of uncertainty, there was no shortage of suitors. My old teammate Ian Stewart wanted

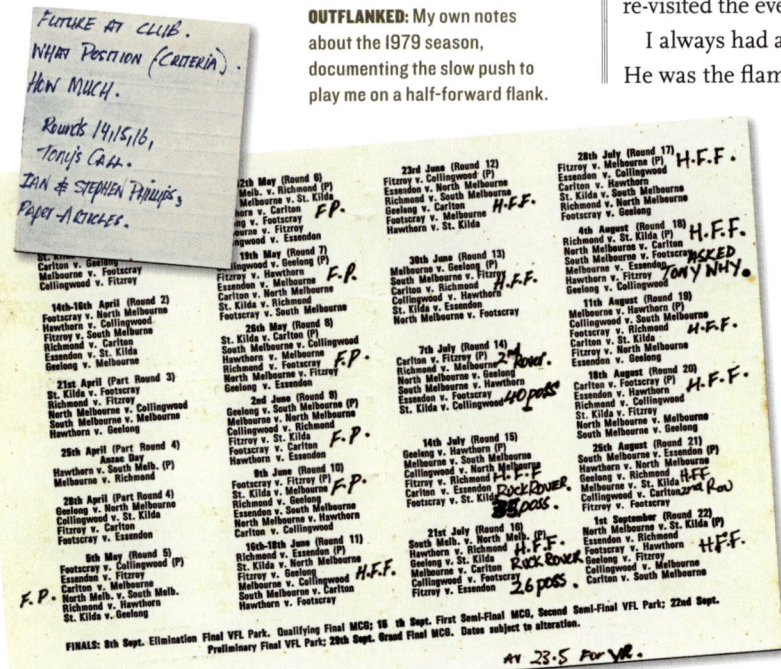

OUTFLANKED: My own notes about the 1979 season, documenting the slow push to play me on a half-forward flank.

BEER BADGE: Carlton defender Geoff Southby closes in on me during the era in which sponsorship logos were just coming in. Michael Roach looks on. At right is an article depicting the passage to my 350th game in round 11, 1981.

me to come to South Melbourne where he was the coach, while Barry Davis was coaching Essendon and wanted me to come to Windy Hill. At Collingwood I met with Tom Hafey, now the Magpies' coach and his long-time assistant, Ron Richards, but Tommy was a bit torn about it all. He said, 'I don't think I could handle taking you away from Richmond'.

I weighed up all the offers. I saw Essendon as a club that could give me the opportunities I wanted and met with Dons committeeman Alan McGillivray. I liked what I heard and then signed a letter of agreement that I would play for the Bombers. I told Tommy the news, but he thought it was the wrong thing to do. So he swayed me to initiate a truce with the Tigers through Michael Green, my great friend and solicitor.

Even though I did sign the letter of agreement with Essendon, deep down, if I were to leave Richmond, I would have gone only to Collingwood with Tom Hafey. But when Tommy told me he felt uncomfortable about the potential move, I had to have a rethink. Tommy is a wise person, someone I admire immensely and whose counsel I seek.

So I took his advice. I told Michael Green, who then approached the board and said that I would return.

As part of the negotiations, the club offered me back the captaincy. But I rejected that because I didn't think at that stage Richmond particularly cared who was captain. Plus I never ever wanted anyone to think that I came back just so I could retain the captaincy.

People may think that perhaps the ghosts of Richmond's past influenced my decision. Barrot had been swapped at the end of the 1970 season. Royce Hart had been forced to retire. Sheeds had been forced to retire. But in the end, it was the counsel of my close friend Tom Hafey that swayed me back to Tigerland. He was right when he told me, 'It would be fantastic for you to finish your career at the one club.'

IN THE SHOP: I meet some fans amid a panoply of memorabilia in Dimmey's department store in Swan Street in celebration of 350th game, in round 11, 1981. Dimmey's, a Richmond institution that was opened in 1853, was painted yellow and black for the occasion.

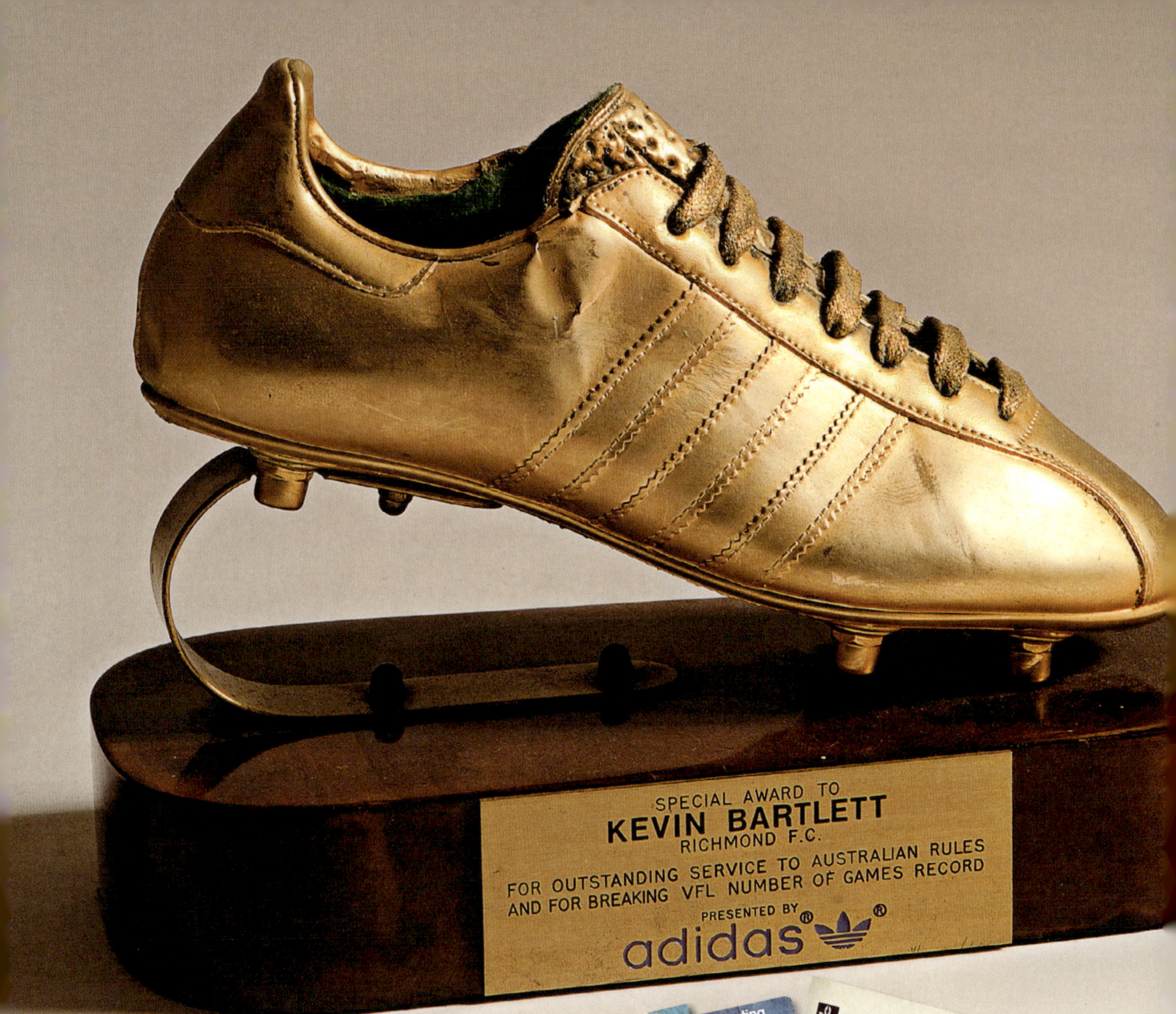

Game Breaker

Ted Whitten was working for adidas when I broke John Rantall's VFL games record of 336 in the qualifying final against Carlton in 1980. Ted had one of my boots gold-plated and he presented it to me. In the letter (far right) from then VFL President Allen Aylett to commemorate the occasion, Aylett lends a personal touch: 'As a former fellow rover, it gives me great pleasure to say well done.' I appreciated his words very much. I also appreciated Teddy's kind telegram.

VICTORIAN FOOTBALL LEAGUE
Dr. ALLEN J. AYLETT . O.B.E.

VFL HOUSE
82 JOLIMONT ST., JOLIMONT
MELBOURNE, VICTORIA, 3002, AUSTRALIA

September 2, 1980

Dear Kevin,

Congratulations on a fantastic effort, I'm sure it will give you tremendous personal satisfaction not only to set a new VFL record for the most number of games played, but to also achieve this honour in a finals game.

To rank on top of the tree of so many famous players is not only a historical achievement but one that reflects a great credit to your undoubted ability as a player your fitness, your dedication and your way of life.

As a former fellow rover it gives me great pleasure to say well done.

Best Wishes,

Yours sincerely,

ALLEN J. AYLETT
PRESIDENT

EGRAM

CONGRATULATIONS KEVIN ON YOUR RECORD BREAKING DAY SATURDAY STOP ALL AT ADIDAS WISH YOU WELL AND ARE PROUD TO HAVE YOU IN OUR TEAM STOP GOOD LUCK IN THE FINALS STOP

REGARDS EJ

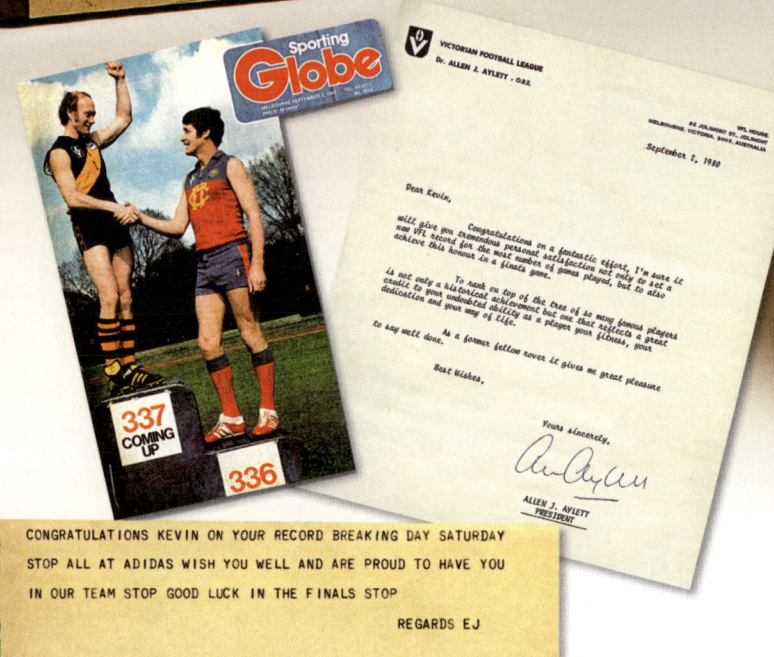

Breaking Jack's Record

This is the football that was used in the game in which I broke Jack Dyer's club record of 310 games (later amended to 312 games) in 1979. 'Captain Blood' hammed it up in front of the lockers for *The Age* (right), and he sent a telegram that I cherish.

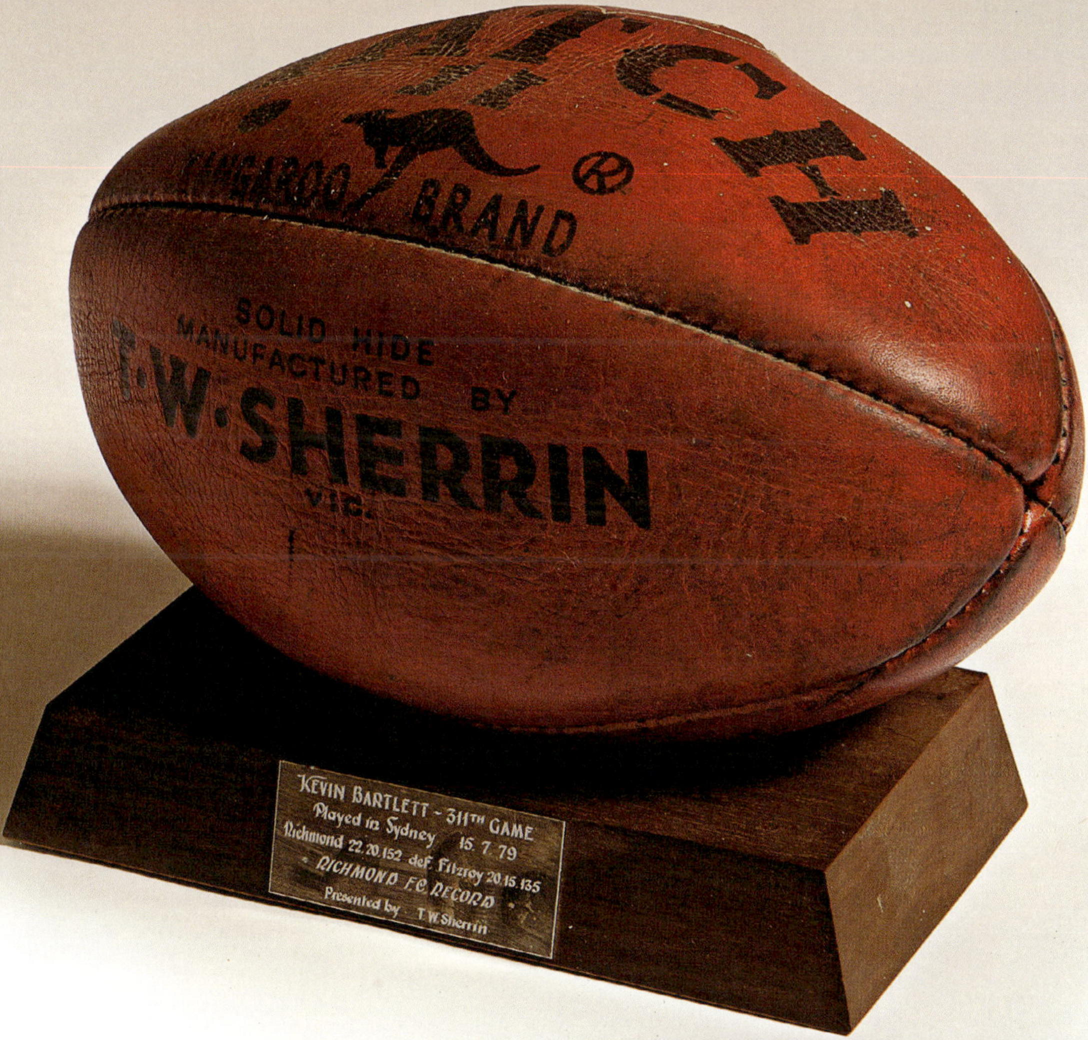

HIGH FIVE: I celebrate my fifth premiership flag.

KB
PLAYING THE GAME

1980 GRAND FINAL

Francis Bourke and I went into the finals keen to push our ageing bodies towards another premiership. It ended up being one of the most satisfying times in our football careers.

We made the finals in 1977 under Barry Richardson. It was Barry's first year. It was a difficult year because Tom Hafey was no longer at Tigerland. We beat South Melbourne in the elimination final and then I kicked four goals in our semi-final loss to North Melbourne, the eventual premier.

Even with that loss in mind, the dream was alive that we could win another Grand Final. We had been a great club for such a long time and I had known only success.

So it was a bit of a shock to miss the finals in 1978 and '79. There was pressure on me as captain in '79 and there was pressure on Tony Jewell in his first year as coach.

In 1979, Richmond finished eighth with only nine wins. I began to think that another premiership was highly unlikely for veterans like me and Francis Bourke. Sheeds was still with us as skills coach. I thought that the parade had passed us by.

That's what made 1980 special.

Francis and I were 33 years old. Only 27 days separated us. And we were about to reach the top one last time. The finals series started off in quirky fashion: Francis and I both played on half-forward flanks in the first two finals. The general feeling was that I was too old to play on the ball and that Francis, the champion wingman, half-back flanker and full-back, was also past his prime.

Consider: our ages combined were 66 years and we were holding up Richmond's half-forward line. It was a great final series for the Tigers – TJ coached

BURNING BRIGHT: A WEG poster and a clipping from *The Sun* herald a special moment.

magnificently. He was able to motivate the players. He brought in Rudi Webster, sports motivator, a man who had been a big influence on the great West Indian cricket teams of the 1970s.

This was something the club hadn't had before. Rudi spoke to the whole group about getting the best out of yourself and controlling your emotions and making certain you don't get over-excited before a match. He was quite a calm, soothing person.

He did hypnosis with certain players. Besides the group gatherings, he saw some players privately, especially those who needed a little more guidance, and those whose confidence needed building.

That's where Tony was terrific as coach – he wasn't afraid to hand over authority to Rudi to work on the players he felt may have needed some more direction.

Many people forget that South Melbourne beat us by 54 points in the last round of the 1980 season. It was a very windy day at the Lake Oval and maybe there were players who, with the finals just around the corner, didn't want to get injured. As a result, we dropped from top spot to third.

So we went into the qualifying final at Waverley Park against Carlton, which had defeated the second-bottom side, Fitzroy, by only four points the previous week. It was a remarkable game for me. Not only was it another finals appearance, but it was my 337th game, breaking John Rantall's League record of games.

I can remember trying to remain extra calm before the game. I was very proud that I had survived so long in the great game of football, and that I was on the verge of breaking the games record. I particularly remember I that had a heightened sense of awareness that I wanted to play well, more than other time in my career.

I didn't want to play poorly in front of a large crowd for a historic match. And I always prided myself on playing very well in finals.

Well, I kicked three goals in the first quarter. I can remember the late Terry Smith kicking the ball to me along the boundary line with a beautiful drop punt that hit me on the chest. I was able to turn around and play on around the boundary line and kick a goal. It was a tremendous boost to the side and myself.

A strange thing happened at quarter-time. The fight between TJ and Carlton coach Percy Jones took place. They were arguing over Rudi, who at one time had been at Carlton. A war of words erupted and the coaches started swinging.

I'll always remember Rudi saying to me afterwards that it was the first time two white men had fought over a black man. I finished up kicking a goal in the second quarter and then a couple in the third quarter. I ended up kicking 6.3 and we ran out easy winners by 42 points.

The next week, in the second semi-final against Geelong, an incident took place that nearly made me miss the 1980 Grand Final. I was waiting under a pack while Jim Jess was following the flight of the ball. He ran into me and we hit heads quite severely and I was for some time.

It could have been much more serious – I could have broken my jaw, Jim could have been more seriously hurt. It was pure luck that we ended up being groggy for only a few minutes. We won that day, by 24 points, and I kicked eight goals straight.

MORE JOY: A *Sporting Globe* front page after the 1980 Grand Final and my Norm Smith Medal.

MORRIS DANCING: I mark in front of former Tiger teammate Kevin Morris during the first half of the 1980 Grand Final.

The 1980 Grand Final against Collingwood is one of the best games I've ever played. A lot of people seem to think I kicked all seven goals on Stan Magro, but that wasn't the case.

My old teammate Kevin Morris actually played on me for the first half. I kicked four goals up to half-time, and then Magro was moved on to me.

I didn't kick a goal in the third quarter, but in the last quarter I kicked three including the much-replayed goal for which I baulked around Magro and kicked a goal from the pocket at the Punt Road end.

Tigers rover Daryl Freame had come off the bench. He kicked the ball out wide to me and I was just able to trap it. I could sense that Stan was right there. As a kid we all practised doing the old fake blind turn, and here came my moment to do that. In fact I had to blind-turn Magro because I was so hard up against the boundary line.

I remember Freame had run on after kicking to me and he was able to shepherd Magro out a bit for me and that gave me space on the boundary line to take bounces and steady before I kicked the goal.

It was a very acute angle, with much room for error. It happened very quickly, but my luck and confidence were sky high. As soon as I kicked the ball I knew it was a goal. It came off the boot so sweetly and straight.

The goal umpire didn't move. I had a chance to kick an eighth goal as the clocked ticked past the 30-minute mark. I wasn't too far out but the ball

BIG WIN: Happy Tigers (from left) Michael Roach, Stephen Mount, Dale Weightman, Geoff Raines, Francis Bourke, Mick Malthouse, Emmett Dunne, Greg Strachan, Daryl Freame, Bryan Wood (obscured), Rob Wiley, David Cloke (obscured), Barry Rowlings and Jim Jess parade the premiership cup.

skewed off my boot and went through the behinds. The crowd booed! I think they regretted that I had missed, because I was only that one goal away from a record eight goals in a Grand Final.

'Good natured hooting,' was how Bobby Skilton explained it on the TV broadcast. "It's the acclamation of how well he has played".

Winning that Grand Final with Francis Bourke beside me was special. It meant that we had played in five of Richmond's 10 winning Grand Finals.

Back row, from left: Rod Oborne, Bruce Tempany, Merv Keane, Greg Strachan, Michael Malthouse, Geoff Raines, Paddy Guinane, Shane Williams, Ian Baker, Robert Wiley, Matthew Wall, Terry Smith. **Third row:** Jim Jess, Emmett Dunne, Colin Waterson, Michael Roach, David Cloke, Mark Lee, Kim Kershaw, Peter Laughlin, Francis Bourke. **Second row:** Bryan Wood, Peter Welsh, Stephen Mount, Richard Doggett (gen man), Bruce Monteath (capt), Ian Wilson (pres), Tony Jewell (coach), Ian Scrimshaw, Graeme Landy, Kevin Bartlett. **Front row:** Daryl Freame, Barry Rowlings, Paul Sarah, Dale Weightman, Dennis Collins, Phil Bottams.

1980 Grand Final
September 27, 1980, MCG

Richmond	6.5	11.11	15.17	**23.21 (159)**
Collingwood	2.6	4.10	5.18	**9.24 (78)**

Best: Richmond – Bartlett, Raines, Lee, Welsh, Bourke, Wiley. **Collingwood** – Woolnough, R. Shaw, Picken, Ohlsen, Davis, Magro.
Goals: Richmond – Bartlett 7, Cloke 6, Wiley 3, Roach 2, Keane 2, Weightman, Jess, Rowlings.
Collingwood – Picken 3, Davis 2, Wearmouth, R. Shaw, Moore, Ohlsen.
Umpires: W. Deller, I. Robinson. **Attendance:** 113,461
Norm Smith Medal: Kevin Bartlett (Rich)

Richmond
B:	M. Malthouse	E. Dunne	G. Strachan
HB:	T. Smith	J. Jess	P. Welsh
C:	S. Mount	G. Raines	B. Wood
HF:	M. Keane	D. Cloke	K. Bartlett
F:	F. Bourke	M. Roach	R. Wiley
R:	M. Lee	B. Rowlings	D. Weightman
Int:	D. Monteath(c)	D. Freame	
Coach:	T. Jewell		

Collingwood
B:	S. Magro	P. McCormack	A. Ireland
HB:	K. Morris	B. Picken	R. Byrne
C:	R. Barham	P. Daicos	L. Carlson
HF:	R. Kink	C. Stewart	I. Low
F:	D. Young	C. Davis	R. Shaw (c)
R:	P. Moore	R. Ohlsen	R. Wearmouth
Int:	T. Shaw	M. Woolnough	
Coach:	T. Hafey		

STARS AND STRIPES: Mark Lee (left), coach Tony Jewell, David Cloke, Geoff Raines and I include the club's tiger skin in the celebrations.

PLAYING THE GAME

THE DAY I WAS REPORTED

Throughout my career, I took pride in being the sort of player who hunted the ball and not the man. It took until 1982, the second last year of my career, for my copybook to be blotted.

I got reported against Geelong at Kardinia Park while playing my 369th game, in round 8, 1982. It was the only time I was reported. My opponent on that day, Bruce Nankervis, was playing a very negative game on me.

He kept hanging on to my guernsey. He put me in a bear hug from behind, and he wrestled me to the ground, all while the ball was a long way away.

I was getting frustrated and I warned Bruce a few times, 'Don't do that Bruce, you don't want to do that. You can play close, but don't keep hanging on to me.'

Bruce continued with the tag and by the third quarter I'd had enough. So I swung around and I whacked him. I hit him in the face, and split his eyebrow open. The solitary field umpire, Neville Nash, saw the incident and reported me.

David Cloke yelled out to Nash, 'You can't report him! You can't report him!' Nash later told me that I said something to the effect of, 'This is partly your fault, Neville,' as he was taking my number. I've heard that in the press conference after the game a journalist told Geelong coach Billy Goggin that "Kevin Bartlett has been reported for striking Bruce Nankervis." Billy is said to have replied, "Well, if that is the case, Neville Nash will get four weeks."

I deserved to be reported because I hit him. It was a risk, but I felt I had no other option. At this stage I was 35 years old. I'd just had enough that day.

When I went along to the tribunal there were many Richmond supporters out the front, waving banners, offering support. There were even a few policemen. The tribunal panel consisted of chairman Jack Gaffney, Brian Bourke and Allan Nash – the uncle of the umpire who reported me!

I reckon Gaffney felt it was significant that I had played 369 games and had never been reported. He figured that someone must have been doing something wrong for me to have turned around and whack somebody. During the case, Neville Nash was answering a question when Brian Bourke leaned over to the other tribunal members and said under his breath, 'Kevin is an ornament to the game.'

When the tribunal asked for my plea, I said, 'Guilty, but not intentional'. I said I had made contact, but I was being hung on to all day. As I swung away to break the tag, I accidentally struck Bruce in the face. That wasn't entirely true, of course, because I really just got sick of him and whacked him. Bruce Nankervis was at the tribunal, but we didn't call him to give evidence. His eyebrow had been stitched up and he didn't look good, so we felt it best not to ask him to give evidence.

I don't think the case went for very long, but I do recall that the verdict came back as 'not guilty'. Neville Nash, some of the tribunal members and I went into the next room and had a soft drink and a chat together. Neville went to leave the tribunal building, but there was that throng of people out the front. I told him to come with me and we could avoid the crowd. We hopped in my car and I drove

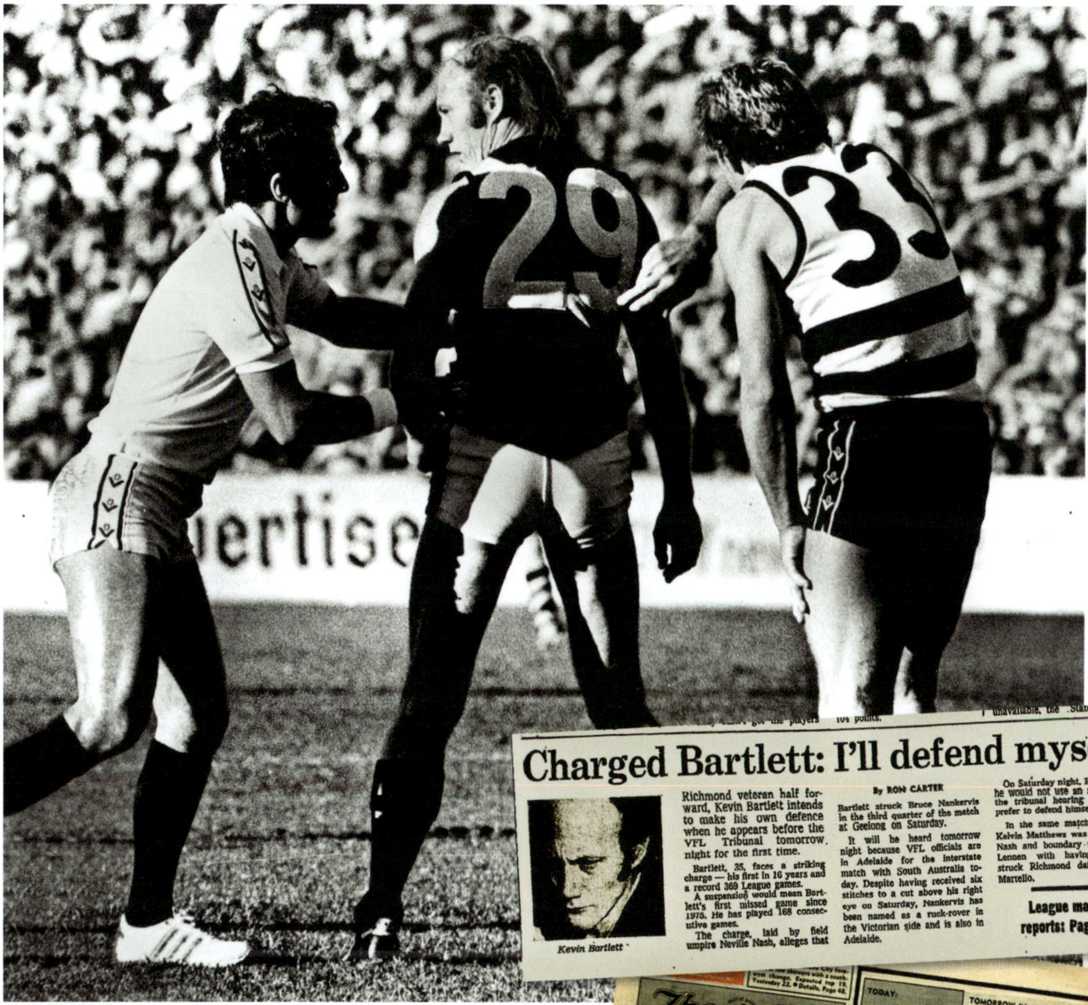

Charged Bartlett: I'll defend myself

Kevin Bartlett

Richmond veteran half forward, Kevin Bartlett intends to make his own defence when he appears before the VFL Tribunal tomorrow night for the first time.

Bartlett, 35, faces a striking charge — his first in 16 years and a record 369 League games.

A suspension would mean Bartlett's first missed game since 1975. He has played 168 consecutive games.

The charge, laid by field umpire Neville Nash, alleges that

By RON CARTER

Bartlett struck Bruce Nankervis in the third quarter of the match at Geelong on Saturday.

It will be heard tomorrow night because VFL officials are in Adelaide for the interstate match with South Australia today. Despite having received six stitches to a cut above his right eye on Saturday, Nankervis has been named as a ruck-rover in the Victorian side and is also in Adelaide.

On Saturday night, Bartlett said he would not use an advocate at the tribunal hearing and would prefer to defend himself.

In the same match, Geelong's Kelvin Matthews was charged by Nash and boundary umpire McLennen with having allegedly struck Richmond defender Alan Martello.

League match reports: Page 24

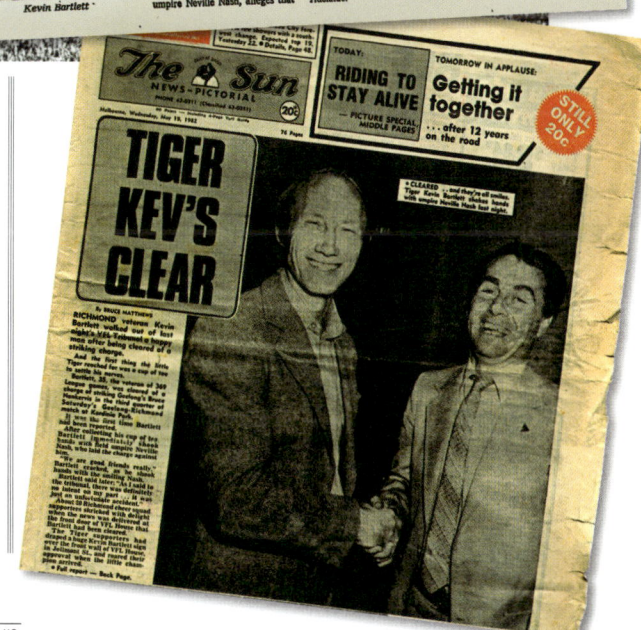

NUMBER'S UP: Umpire Neville Nash reports me after seeing me strike Bruce Nankervis (No.33) in round 8, 1982. It was my first report in 369 games. I pleaded "guilty but not intentional" and got off, as you can see from the clippings.

The Sun NEWS-PICTORIAL

20c

TODAY: RIDING TO STAY ALIVE — PICTURE SPECIAL, MIDDLE PAGES

TOMORROW IN APPLAUSE: Getting it together ... after 12 years on the road

STILL ONLY 20c

TIGER KEV'S CLEAR

By BRUCE MATTHEWS

RICHMOND veteran Kevin Bartlett walked out of last night's VFL Tribunal a happy man after being cleared of a striking charge.

And the first thing the little Tiger reached for was a cup of tea to settle his nerves.

Bartlett, 35, the veteran of 369 League games, was cleared of a charge of striking Geelong's Bruce Nankervis in the third quarter of Saturday's Geelong-Richmond match at Kardinia Park.

It was the first time Bartlett had been reported.

After collecting his cup of tea Bartlett immediately shook hands with field umpire Neville Nash, who laid the charge against him.

"We are good friends really," Bartlett cracked, as he shook hands with the smiling Nash.

Bartlett said later: "As I said to the tribunal, there was definitely no intent on my part ... it was just an unfortunate accident."

About 20 Richmond cheer squad supporters shrieked with delight when the news was delivered at the front door of VFL House that Bartlett had been cleared.

The Tiger supporters had draped a huge Kevin Bartlett sign over the front wall of VFL House, in Jolimont St., and roared their approval when the little champion arrived.

• Full report — Back Page.

• CLEARED ... and they're all smiles. Tiger Kevin Bartlett shakes hands with umpire Neville Nash last night.

him around to his car out the front. I have seen Bruce Nankervis and Neville Nash many times since and we have a laugh and a joke about that incident. Bruce himself admits that his tactics were out of line considering the ball was more than 50 metres away.

There was a celebration a few days after my 400th game and Bruce Nankervis and Billy Goggin came along. So there were no hard feelings at all. Bruce, who played 253 games for the Cats, should have just heeded my warning that day at Kardinia Park.

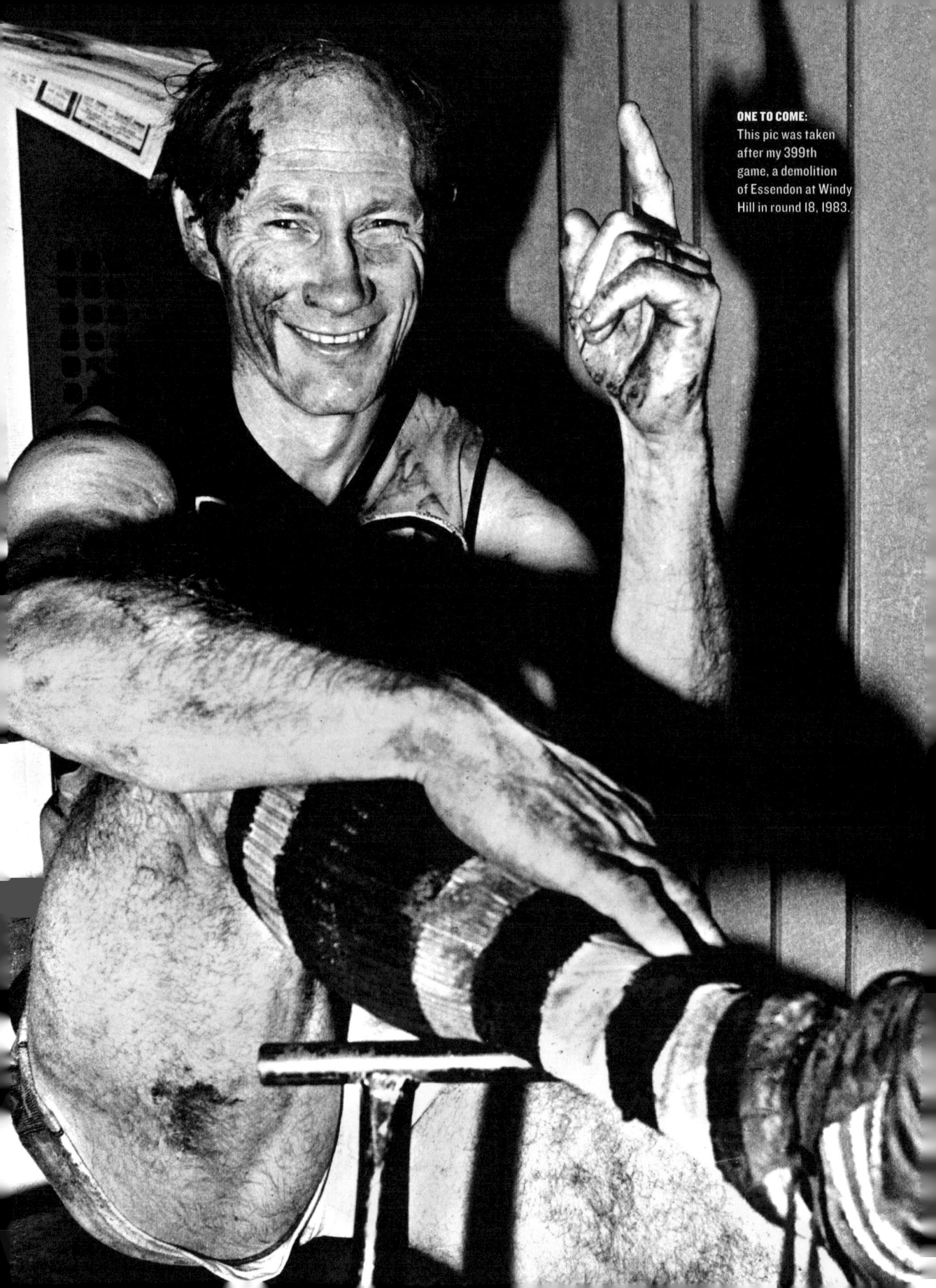

ONE TO COME: This pic was taken after my 399th game, a demolition of Essendon at Windy Hill in round 18, 1983.

KB
PLAYING THE GAME

THE TRIP TO 400 GAMES

The lead-up included receiving the key to the city and racing Jack Dyer during a trots meeting at Moonee Valley. The only hurdle was the banner before the game.

It was the man who opened the door for me the very first time I went to Punt Road who planted the seed for me to play 400 games of League football. Bill Boromeo sent me a congratulatory note after I played my 300th game, but it was this footnote to his lovely letter – 'Why not 400?' – that struck a chord with me.

I read it as a challenge: to continue to play on and to continue to enjoy playing. It was unthinkable at the time for someone to play 400 games. But that question, posed by a lifelong friend and mentor, gave me the impetus to try.

The lead-up to my 400th game in round 19 1983 was tremendous. My 399th game was against Essendon at Windy Hill and I was photographed in the rooms after the game holding up one finger, as if to say, 'one more game'. That photo was used in the papers throughout the week to build up the game.

For the whole week, there were radio, press and TV interviews as well as functions to attend. Ron Yates was a great Richmond supporter and coterie member who had a yellow Rolls-Royce. He picked me up on the Wednesday morning and chauffeured me to the City Square, where the Lord Mayor presented me with the keys to the City of Melbourne. A huge crowd had turned up and I had brought my whole family with me. I received the large key while wearing a Four'N Twenty branded pullover, as the pie company was sponsoring me at the time.

In addition, the Dimmey's Clocktower in Swan Street, Richmond, a famous Melbourne landmark, was painted yellow and black in my honour. To this day it still has those colours. Dimmey's is only a stone's throw away from the house I'd grown up in.

On the night before my 400th game, I had a match-race against Jack Dyer during the harness racing meeting at Moonee Valley. Rather than

LONG INNINGS: At right and below is 400th game memorabilia.

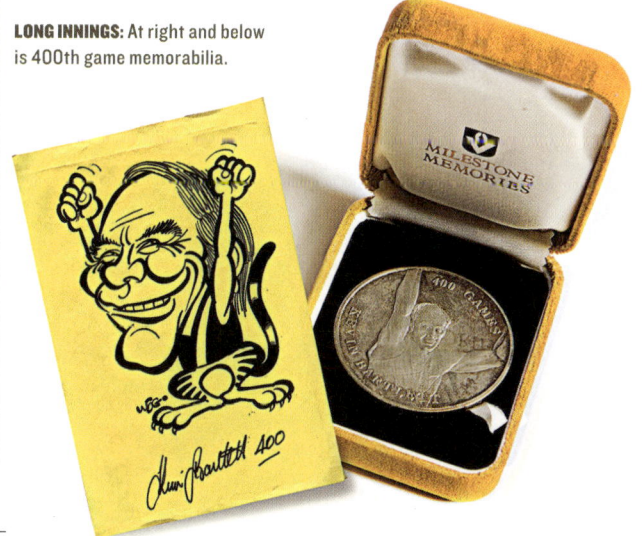

BIG PICTURE: Denise, Francis Bourke, Roger Dean and Tom Hafey sign a caricature of me, as drawn by renowned artist Brian Clinton.

HOT TO TROT: Jack Dyer and I (above) pace ourselves at Moonee Valley on the night before my 400th milestone; and (right) two of the more rustic mementoes.

relaxing at home, having fish and chips and cups of tea, resting and preparing for the big day, I was at the Valley, wearing my lace-up jumper opposite Jack, who was dressed in silks. To this day, I have no idea what it was for. We were to do a full lap of the course. I remember that Jack took off like lightning! He was fearless. He must have had some driving experience because he was taking it very seriously. I made up some ground in the straight but I didn't want to go full speed, fall out of the sulky and injure myself on the night before my biggest game. Jack beat me in a photo finish.

Looking back, it was such a stupid thing for me to do the night before such a big event.

On the morning of my 400th game, I was calm but any thoughts that it would be just a game were dashed by the size of the crowd at the MCG, which was of finals proportions. It was quite amazing when you consider that Richmond was out of finals contention and Collingwood had no more than a reasonable chance of making the finals. Before the

THE BIG DAY: Finally, I run out to play my 400th, against Collingwood in round 19, 1983. My teammate are (from left) Michael Roach, Phil Egan, Merv Keane, Greg Conlan, David Palm, Dale Weightman, Jim Jess, Greg Strachan, Neil Peart (obscured), Robert Wiley and Dan Foley.

game, I received a large card that the Collingwood players had signed to congratulate me on my achievement, which was a nice touch.

The banner was 10 metres high and 20 metres long. It had taken 500 hours to make and it cost $400. David Norman, the cheer squad leader, had overseen its creation. It took 29 cheer squad members to hold up the banner. I had actually seen the banner a few days earlier. I was down at the club. The cheer squad put up the banner and I had some photos in front of it. I remember saying, 'Gee it looks big and strong, how am I going to get through it?' and Norman pointing out to me the 'weak' spots they had put in the banner for me to run through. Maybe he pointed to the wrong part of the banner, or maybe I didn't listen as well as I should have.

As many people remember, I ran down the race with teammates on either side of me, VFL general manager Jack Hamilton and club president Ian Wilson applauding me, and television cameras at the base of the banner. I picked up speed and ran into it, but I couldn't get through and fell flat on my face. So I just bounced up off the ground and kept running. I've always maintained that they forgot to tell me that there was a large piece of wood across the bottom, which was stabilising the banner, Running through that banner was like running through a brick wall. It could have been the end of my 400th game then and there. My opponent was Ray Byrne, a half-back flanker who was a bit of a character. He had a comb in his sock that had no teeth and he presented it to me. I don't know what happened to it, but perhaps I threw it on the ground in disgust. He thought it was a bit of fun.

My 400th game was fair, nothing more than that. I was at the end of my career and my body and mind had just about had it. I ended up with 16 kicks and six marks and we lost the game, but the day as a whole was a great thrill for me.

Nobody had every played 400 games before. Most previous record-holders had reached 300 games or the current League games record, played one more

GUARD OF HONOUR: The fanfare over my 400th game reached its peak when I ran on to the ground. Some of those who lined up are (from left) players Trevor Poole and Michael Lockman, trainer Ray Webb and team manager Trevor Lorrins. In the officials' line are (from right) VFL general manager Ian Hamilton, Richmond president Ian Wilson, Richmond benefactor David Mandie, prominent Richmond supporter Peter Nixon, former Victorian premier Lindsay Thompson and leading businessman John Knott.

GAME TIME: Collingwood's Ray Byrne (left), teammate Michael Roach and Craig Stewart keep me company during my 400th.

game and then that was it. I think I broke the League record by the greatest number of games ever. It was 336 when I reached it and I ended up playing 403 – 67 games more than the previous record.

I was pleased I got to 400 because I felt it would be a great incentive for other players to play on. There was always talk that when players got to 300 they were at the end of their career, but I didn't buy that. I was saying that when you get into your mid-30s, if you're still enthusiastic about the game then you should continue to play. It doesn't matter if the media think your time is up. If your enthusiasm is there and you have the support of the club, then keep playing.

I am a surprised that the great Hawthorn champion Michael Tuck is the only other player to have reached 400 games because in this modern era, with superior training and increased medical support, the milestone seems attainable for a full-time footballer.

I expect that we should see more players passing the 400-game milestone in the coming decades, especially as there are more rotations. In theory you don't play a full game these days because everyone gets rotated off the ground at some stage, midfielders particularly so.

We will see. At the time of writing, the player closest to 400 is Essendon's Dustin Fletcher, who at the age of 36 had played 328 games. To reach 400 games he's need to play until he was 40. Perhaps the number is further away than we might imagine. In my time, I was on the field for the whole game – 403 times over, unless I was dragged or injured.

After the 400th game, there was a party back at the house of coterie supporter Bruce Gough, with some 200 of my closest friends. Newspapers covered the event. A gorilla-gram turned up, but Dale Weightman threw him into the swimming pool, so the poor man had to dry his gorilla suit in the clothes dryer. I don't think he cared in the end because he stayed for the whole party.

The next day at Punt Road, the club held a huge afternoon for supporters, where fans could have a photograph taken with me for $2. Later on, there was a function at the Regent Hotel in the city.

K.B. 400

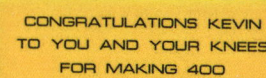
CONGRATULATIONS KEVIN TO YOU AND YOUR KNEES FOR MAKING 400
CASEY & DANNY

KIND WORDS: There were plenty of headlines surrounding my 400th game. Also included here are much appreciated telegrams from Ron Barassi and one of Richmond's top administrators, Alan Schwab.

MORE HOOPLA: The kids were keen to join in the fun over my 400th. At left and below are commemorations of my career: the WEG poster (left) and number plate (below).

Tickets cost $100 each and it was packed. Many friends and people from my past got up to speak. I remember that Mike Williamson interviewed my mother, which was a first for her. There were musical acts and comedians. Mike Brady of *Up There Cazaly* fame had written a new song about my career called *Hungry*, which he played.

The following week we played St Kilda in my 401st game and I kicked 2.3. It was the last time I kicked a goal in League football. My 402nd game was against Sydney at the MCG where I had just one kick and one handball. I was on the bench for the whole game until very late in the last quarter. It was the last winning game of football I played in.

And then came my last game. Hardly anyone knows this story. In the week leading up to my 403rd and last game for Richmond I tore my quad muscle in my right leg at training early in the week. I swore the club doctor to secrecy because there was no way I was going to miss this game. So on the Thursday night before my last training session he gave me a couple of jabs in my leg. I was able to get through training but it was very sore the next day and I was unable to lift my leg.

I needed a couple of jabs to get out there for my final game. My leg was OK for the first half but after half-time my thigh muscle was shot. I stayed on but it was very difficult to run and if I got the ball it was pretty hard to kick it. I ended my career with 10 kicks, four marks and four behinds. I was 36 years 174 days old. My journey was over.

By the time of my retirement I was able to take a moment and look back at my career. Sadly, my first two coaches, Len Smith and Jack Titus, had both passed on. My first opponent, St Kilda's Daryl Griffiths, had been retired for 13 years. Tom Hafey had entered our lives as coach and left a legacy of four premierships. I no longer had as much hair on my head. A lace-up jumper had replaced long, woollen jumpers. And I finished my 19 seasons of football by appearing on the MCG for the 200th time. It was the same ground on which I'd started my career, way back in 1965.

TWO'S COMPANY: A line was coined that you could fill the MCG with the players who've played 200 games, but you could only fill a phone booth with those to have played 400. Well, here I am with Michael Tuck in a phone booth. Thanks for calling! The photo was shot for the *AFL Record* for the 2010 Grand Final.

Almost Front Page News

In late September 1983, just a few weeks after my final game, The Sun asked whether I would pose for a picture on the front page with Rhett. The idea was that I was the League's record games holder and a five-time premiership player and that September was my time of year. So we met photographer John Casamento and we did the shot. That evening I got a phone call from the editor saying they had printed the front page of their newspaper and there was a problem. There was a large ad for cigarettes at the bottom of the page and it was considered inappropriate to have a young child on the front page seemingly endorsing cigarettes. My understanding was that around 580,000 copies of that front page were pulped. However, because the newspaper people felt awful about what had happened, they sent 10 copies for me to keep as a memento. And so I have in my possession a lovely colour front page of The Sun from Friday, September 23, 1983 that has never been seen in public. Until now.

Premiership Medals

The premiership medals are a constant reminder of the golden era of the Richmond Football Club. I played in five premierships, but I have six medals. I received the medals on the see-through stand a few weeks after the five Grand Final victories. Those medals have the premiership side written on the back. By 1980, premiership players were receiving medallions on the dais after the game. So in 1980 I received a medal on a stand as well as the premiership medal. I hold all of my medals close to my heart.

KB
PLAYING THE GAME

MY BEST RICHMOND TEAM

How many former players could choose a line-up of former teammates to match this one? Not many. It's full of champions, and has a rare blend of skill and toughness.

What a task! Coming up with the best team of teammates over a 19-season career! While I sweated over my selections, it's no surprise that I ended up with a rare blend of skill and toughness.

The best Richmond teams have featured these traits since Dan Minogue led the Tigers to our first premierships in the early 1920s and Checker Hughes and Perc Bentley came up with winning formulas a decade later. The team is versatile: witness the inclusion of Barry Richardson and Dick Clay. It's shrewd: Kevin Sheedy takes care of that. You might think that Neil Balme lends a brutal edge, but he had his subtleties. You don't win premierships if you can't put some thought into the way you play.

Of course, the difficulty was who to leave out. I could easily have chosen Geoff Strang in a back flank role. He was a dasher and a great kick and a proven big game player.

John Northey could have been selected on the half forward flank. "Swooper" played that role superbly as an opportunist and was a great tackler.

Graham Burgin also just missed out. He was a tough, quick defender who was a major player in our 1967 and 1969 Premiership side. Sadly, injury limited his career.

Some other players who were close to selection include Brian Roberts. 'The Whale' was not only an outstanding ruckman but his huge personality helped galvanise the club. And Bill Brown, my little roving mate from the 1967 and 1969 Premierships was so courageous and could kick that important goal.

Paul Sproule was a clever rover and forward pocket. His nous set up many goals for the Tigers.

Still, I'm happy with what I've chosen. How couldn't you be? Every time I ran on to the ground in a Richmond jumper I felt proud to play alongside such talented and devoted footballers.

Tom Hafey encouraged all his players to get the most out of themselves. Looking at this team, he would be very happy with the results.

Kevin Bartlett's Best R.F.C. Team (1965-83)

COACH
Tom Hafey

RUCKS
Michael Green
Bill Barrot
Dale Weightman

BACKS
Kevin Sheedy — Barry Richardson — Jim Jess

HALF-BACKS
Mervyn Keane — Robert McGhie — Francis Bourke (vc)

CENTRES
Dick Clay — Ian Stewart — Geoff Raines

HALF-FORWARDS
Roger Dean (c) — Royce Hart — Maurice Rioli

FORWARDS
Robert Wiley — Michael Roach — Neil Balme

INTERCHANGE
David Cloke
Wayne Walsh
Kevin Morris
Bryan Wood

EMERGENCIES
Mark Lee
Barry Rowlings
Bruce Monteath

Back Pocket
Kevin Sheedy
Games for Richmond: 251 (1967-79)
Goals: 91

Kevin Sheedy and I first met when we were 10 years old, having a kick in the park, along with his brother Pat. I then went to live in Richmond and played with the Richmond under-17s, while 'Sheeds' lived in South Yarra and played for Prahran.

He and I finished up in the same school football team together, at Prahran Tech, and he also sold papers up at the hotel that my father would frequent, so I would see him up there all the time.

I don't think there has been a better back-pocket player than Kevin Sheedy. He was innovative, cunning and antagonistic – mouthing off the opposition, falling on top of them when he took a mark, or scragging them to the ground, and it generally worked a treat. His opponents would give away silly free kicks; Sheeds could act as though he had been poleaxed when an opponent touched him. He was an extremely smart player and worked the angles very well. He actually was quite skilful, although Tommy Hafey was more intent on the players kicking the ball a lot longer and deeper. Sheeds got into a bit of trouble because Tommy reckoned he was a little too fancy.

Ever alert to possibilities, he would do look-away handpasses, such as during the 1974 Grand Final when he ran in to have a shot for goal from 20 metres but instead handballed over the man on the mark to Michael Green in the goalsquare. He was always looking for something different.

Full-Back
Barry Richardson
Games for Richmond: 125 (1965-74)
Goals: 134

The first time I saw Barry was in 1964, when Richmond was playing South Melbourne in a night game at the Lake Oval. We were getting ready in the rooms and in walked this very thin, gangly kid with blond hair. He had been brought down from St Pat's Ballarat. Barry had an ungainly gait and he looked a bit meek but he turned out to be extremely tough. His angelic looks defied a mean competitive streak.

One of his main traits was versatility. He played on a half-forward flank in the 1967 Grand Final and in 1969 he played at full-back on Alex Jesaulenko. 'Jezza' was a superstar at the time but 'Bones', as we called him, kept the Blues spearhead to one goal.

He then missed 1973 with a knee injury but in the 1974 Grand Final he played at full-forward and kicked five goals. He played in three positions in three winning Grand Finals. What a player!

Besides being a ferocious competitor, Barry brought some skill to the full-back position. He was a beautiful kick rather than your typical mongrel-punting full-back. He also kept Peter Hudson goalless for the first time in 'Huddo's' career, in round 7, 1969. Barry was able to always read the play. Rather than stand around and wait for the full-forward to make the first move, he often moved first and reached the ball before his opponent.

The fact that he was so proactive puts him in my best Richmond team ever.

Back Pocket
Jim Jess
Games for Richmond: 223 (1976-88)
Goals: 175

I have always been a huge fan of Jumping Jim, who was just as versatile as Bones Richardson. 'The Ghost', as we called him, dominated at centre half-forward in the 1980 Grand Final, but he could also play at full-forward and centre half-back and he could mind the resting ruckmen in a back pocket. He really was a Mr Fix-It type.

Ghost was very quick, particularly in a straight line, and he was a sensational mark, as brave as they came. In the 1980 final series, he took a towering grab in the goalsquare against Geelong in the second semi-final at Waverley. His mark helped seal the game for the Tigers. The trait for which he's

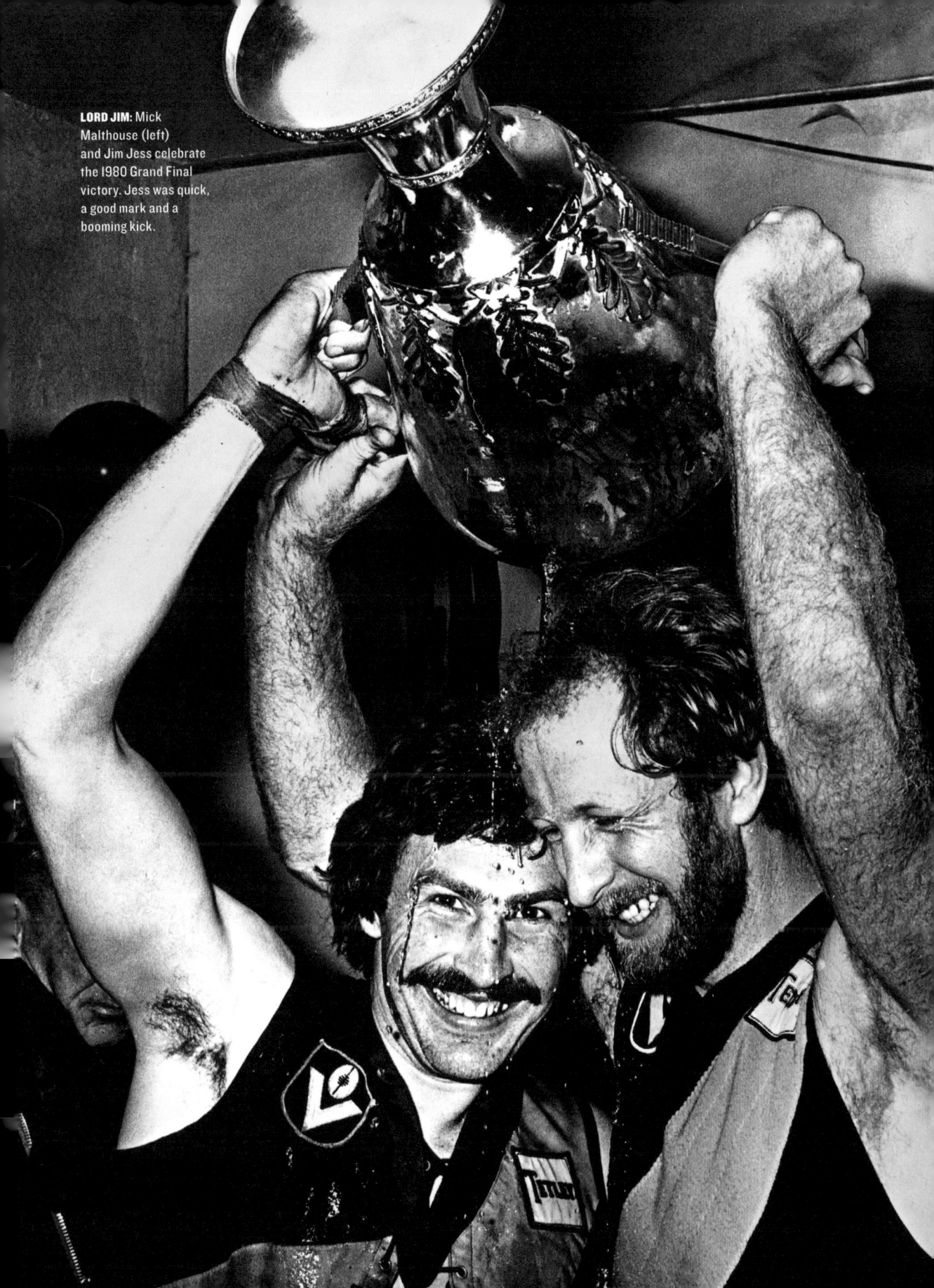

LORD JIM: Mick Malthouse (left) and Jim Jess celebrate the 1980 Grand Final victory. Jess was quick, a good mark and a booming kick.

most remembered is his ability to boot booming torpedoes. He was forever practising them at training. The first time I ever saw Jimmy was one night at training in 1976. He had come down from St Arnaud. He had a pale face, blond hair all over the joint, and he jumped over everyone to take these huge marks during kick-to-kick. I stood there thinking to myself, 'Who the hell is that bloke taking marks over Royce Hart?'

His wonderful career at Richmond started that evening and he went on to become a club great and a deserved inductee into Richmond's Hall of Fame.

Half-Back Flank
Mervyn Keane
Games for Richmond: 238 (1972-84)
Goals: 36

On his first night of training, Merv Keane was directed towards a group of players, so he ran over and joined in. It wasn't until the group of players started returning to the MCG rather than Punt Road that he realised he'd just trained with Melbourne! It was to Richmond's lasting benefit that Merv found his way to Tigerland. He was a half-back who just kept beating his opponent, week in, week out.

He was an exceptionally strong mark for his size. He had a strong centre of gravity and he held his feet. He wasn't flashy, nor exceptionally quick, and nor did he take skyscraping marks; he just beat quality opponents with monotonous regularity.

He played the half-back flank almost his entire career. In the 1980 Grand Final he made a rare foray out of the backline, at least for a while, when he played as ruck-rover, changing at half-back with Terry Smith. He ended up playing 248 games for the Tigers and was selected in the Team of the Century.

Centre Half-Back
Robert McGhie
Games for Richmond: 81 (1973-78)
Goals: 0

Robbie was 190cm, could run like the wind and, despite an ungainly kicking action, all his kicks were long and effective. He had very long arms and he was a fine exponent of Richmond's game-plan, which was to run fast, get the ball and kick it as far as possible. He was as mean and nasty as he looked with all those tattoos, and he roughed opponents up. But at the same time, he was effective with the ball.

Tom Hafey got him to Richmond after meeting Robbie's mother in a shop in Footscray. Apparently, Robbie's mother introduced herself and told Tommy that Rob had left Footscray and wasn't doing much. Tom went to see him and convinced him to come to Tigerland. Tommy had always had his eye on Robbie while he played at Footscray. He often said he loved the fact that Robbie was quick and wiry, and able to kick the ball a country mile.

Half-Back Flank
Francis Bourke
Games for Richmond: 300 (1967-81)
Goals: 71

I first saw Francis when he came down to play in the reserves. Before finding his niche on a wing and across half-back, his first few senior games were as my second rover. He then went on to become the greatest wingman to ever play the game. He was picked on the wing in the AFL's Team of the Century, but given that he was just as effective at half-back he gets my nod there.

With his unselfishness, single-mindedness and competitiveness, he was second to no one as a defender. No one played tougher, harder and more straight down the line than Francis. He was a strong mark, a long kick and he was fast without being super quick. He was a ferocious competitor and nothing could sap his concentration.

So many times I can recall him grabbing the ball, beating his opponent, running down the ground and kicking long, then turning around and sprinting as hard as he could to get back to his man. He always put great store in beating his opponent. Francis was a tremendous leader, always giving directions, always helping the team by calling players back and marshalling the troops. He was a superstar.

TIGERS OF OLD: Francis Bourke and I celebrate our second semi-final victory over Geelong in 1980, putting us through to another Grand Final.

Wing
Dick Clay
Games for Richmond: 213 (1966-76)
Goals: 80

Any discussion about Dick Clay needs to start with the fact he could have been named in this team as full-back, because he played in that position in a Grand Final. Clay was one of the most versatile players I played with.

At Kyabram he played full-forward. In his first game for Richmond he played at centre half-forward on Ted Whitten and was voted best on ground. Getting him to Richmond was one of the club's finest recruiting coups because he was all but certain to join North Melbourne before we pinched him at the last minute.

Tommy Hafey moved him on to the wing, because he loved the idea of a tall wingman who was quick and a big kick. Dick was a very good mark; in fact he was one of the best all-round talented footballers ever to play at Richmond. Dick played a wonderful game in the 1973 Grand Final at full-back on Jesaulenko, but moved back to the wing the following year when Barry Richardson came back to the team. Not too many opponents beat Dick on the wing.

He was always very enthusiastic about the Tigers and his passion for the club has long been evident. He supports the club through thick and thin.

Centre
Ian Stewart
Games for Richmond: 78 (1971-75)
Goals: 55

This was a toss-up between Ian Stewart and Bill Barrot. Both were great centreman in my era, but I've put 'Stewie' ahead of Barrot, because Billy played the centre position more like a ruck-rover: he ran all over the place and he was a goalkicker as well.

In my eyes, Ian was more your purist's centreman. He was a craftsman who had lovely timing with his kicking and I don't think anyone his size has been a better mark. He was truly a legendary player, and I doubt you could name a better centreman to have ever played the game.

It was a massive story when the pair swapped clubs in 1971. Barrot was a Richmond hero, a dual premiership player, while Stewart was a dual Brownlow Medalist at St Kilda. He joined Richmond feeling he had a point to prove. He wanted to show St Kilda that he wasn't washed up and he worked really hard to demonstrate that he wasn't a poor trainer, which was the reputation he brought with him from Moorabbin.

When he came to Richmond in 1971 I think it's fair to say that he trained harder than he ever had. He was on a mission to re-establish himself as a star of the game. In the short time he was at Richmond, he won a premiership, a best and fairest and his third Brownlow Medal in 1971.

Wing
Geoff Raines
Games for Richmond: 134 (1976-82)
Goals: 53

Geoff Raines played his first half a dozen games as my second rover, so I saw him develop from a young player into a star. He was a beautiful kick and a wonderful mover with his low centre of gravity, but he was also was as tough as an old tree.

It's not a quality that many would ascribe to him, but Geoff would crash into packs, crunch players and take heavy knocks. He earned the 'Pretty Boy' nickname because he was a good-looking player with blow-waved hair, but it was a misleading nickname in terms of his football.

I witnessed him up close. He was hard at the ball and not frightened to mix it with anyone.

Geoff was at Richmond for only seven seasons. In that time he won three best and fairests, including one in a premiership year, in 1980. I think it is one of the great tragedies of the club that he left us to go to Collingwood in 1983. He was one of the best players I ever played with.

DESTINY: Captain Roger Dean is confident as he leads the Tigers down the race before the 1969 Grand Final. Behind him is vice-captain Royce Hart. Both are members of my best team.

Half-Forward Flank
Roger Dean
Games for Richmond: 245 (1957-73)
Goals: 204

Roger Dean was the most loved player during my time at Richmond. Every teammate adored him and admired him. He was at Tigerland for 10 seasons before we all came along to help win the 1967 premiership. Roger played in the back pocket in 1967 premiership win over Geelong. Everyone seems to remember Fred Swift's great match-saving mark in the last quarter, but everyone forgets that Roger Dean took a courageous mark right on the goal-line as well. He was an extraordinary mark.

He was a star with Richmond through all the junior grades, a half-forward flanker who went back to the back pocket and then moved back to the half-forward line. Unprecedented. Off the field he was the quietest and most thoughtful person you could ever meet, but as soon as he ran down the race he became a dynamo. When he put on the No.3 Richmond jumper, it was like Clark Kent changing into Superman.

He was ferocious with his attack on the ball and he wasn't frightened to hand out a bit of biffo. I'm certain Kevin Sheedy copied Roger's antagonistic manner. Roger was a master at getting 15-metre penalties. He would have the ball and be running towards goal but rather than kick the ball, he held on to it until the very last second so he would get crunched just as he was kicking. The umpire had to pay a free kick down the field. It shows you how tough he was: deliberately getting hit, as he was about to kick.

Winning the 1969 premiership with Roger Dean as our captain is one of my career highlights.

Centre Half-Forward
Royce Hart
Games for Richmond: 187 (1967-77)
Goals: 369

In my opinion, Royce Hart is the greatest centre half-forward the game has seen. Royce was a star from the very first game he played, so much so that he played for Victoria after just seven games for Richmond. Then to emphasise his talent, he kicked seven goals in that game.

He was the first League footballer in my era to be able to mark by floating across the front of a pack. In those days players used to kick the ball long to packs. Ruckmen dropped back all the time to contest, but Royce would outmark them. And it wasn't like he was taking easy little marks like they do today; his marks were big, important and always spectacular.

Sometimes I would watch and think to myself, 'There is no way he is going to make that pack in time.' Yet he managed to hang in the air and float towards the ball. Although a poor kick on his right foot, he was a magnificent long kick on his left. He was very quick and if he was playing in the modern game now, he would most likely be playing in the midfield. He was also a great tackler. So while a lot of players would try to beat him in the air, he was almost unbeatable when the ball was on the ground.

Half-Forward Flank
Maurice Rioli
Games for Richmond: 118 (1982-87)
Goals: 80

I played only two years with Maurice but in that time he showed enough to ensure his selection in my best Richmond team. He won the best and fairest in 1982 and '83 and was also runner-up in the Brownlow Medal in '83. His evasive skills and his tackling skills bought a new dimension to the club.

He had a sixth sense, knowing the whereabouts of opposition players, sidestepping at just the right time to create extra space. And he was a beautiful left-foot kick. He had a very low centre of gravity, so he never lost his footing, and he didn't fumble. Great players don't fumble. I've got four champion centremen in this team: Ian Stewart, Bill Barrot, Geoff Raines and Maurice Rioli. None of them can miss out. Maurice could play half-forward flank, or take a run in the centre. In today's game, you would play him on the ball. He was just so good.

HIGH TIMES: Robert Wiley celebrates with me after a goal during the 1982 second semi-final against Carlton at Waverley Park.

Forward Pocket
Robert Wiley
Games for Richmond: 95 (1979-83)
Goals: 128

Robert won five best and fairests at the Perth Football Club before coming to Richmond and another three with Perth *after* he left Richmond. His eight best-player awards show just what a champion player he was. He was 24 when he came to Tigerland in 1979 and it was clear from the start that he was a ball magnet.

He was an outstanding rover and a brilliant forward, with equal ability on either foot and a League average of a goal a game.

Rob finished runner-up in the 1980 and '81 Richmond best-and-fairest counts and came third in '82. We had him for only five seasons but he was a great Richmond player in that time.

In particular, his 1980 final series was magnificent – he averaged 28 disposals a game. He always knew where the ball was going and he never fumbled. He actually ended up taking my on-ball position; it was partly because of Rob's talents that the club moved me to the half-forward flank.

As a side note, we finished our Richmond careers on the same day, the final home and away game of 1983, against Fitzroy at the MCG.

Full-Forward
Michael Roach
Games for Richmond: 200 (1977-89)
Goals: 607

When Michael first started, he was a tall and skinny wingman who played a handful of senior games.

He was insignificant in the scheme of things. It wasn't until 1979, his third season, that he was moved to the forward line and he kicked 90 goals.

Roach is the best Richmond full-forward I have seen. He was unstoppable for a few years and complemented our side magnificently. I had the best seat in the house to see him take one of the truly great marks ever, his breathtaking leap over the heads of a number of Hawthorn players at the MCG in round five of 1979.

He had a terrific pair of hands and followed it up with his beautiful kicking action. In fact, I rate him as the best kick for goal I have seen and would back him against anyone.

He kicked 607 goals in 200 games and when you consider that injury kept him to just 10 senior games out of a possible 44 games in his final two seasons, his return in front of goals when fully fit was extraordinary.

It was a mistake by the club to leave 'Roachy' out of Richmond's Team of the Century and I'm still staggered he was overlooked. Matthew Richardson had played only six years in the AFL by that stage. His selection was premature. Compare Richardson's first six years to Roach's career and there is no comparison.

Forward Pocket
Neil Balme
Games for Richmond: 159 (1969-79)
Goals: 229

Neil is one of the most talented big men I have seen. I'm not sure there has ever been a guy of his size who could kick so well with both sides of his body, snap goals from both sides, unleash a booming kick and take such great marks.

I'm greatly disappointed when people focus on Neil's fighting and the ruthlessness he showed against Geoff Southby and Vin Waite in the 1973 Grand Final. In terms of talent, ball-handling and agility he was unbelievable. Unfortunately, chronic knee soreness dimmed his star towards the end of his career.

Neil was a great teammate because no opponents ever gave me lip if 'Balmey' was near. Defenders would shake in their boots when he walked down to the forward line, which was a nice twist on the normal course of events, as defenders are normally the aggressors in these situations.

I didn't like to be in any Richmond team without Balmey by my side.

BEST OF ALL: I reckon Michael Roach's mark over a tangle of Hawthorn players is the greatest mark in football. And given that I had a front-row view, I should know! Roach took the mark in round five, 1979. The Hawthorn players visible are Terry Moore (front) and Kelvin Moore (long sleeves).

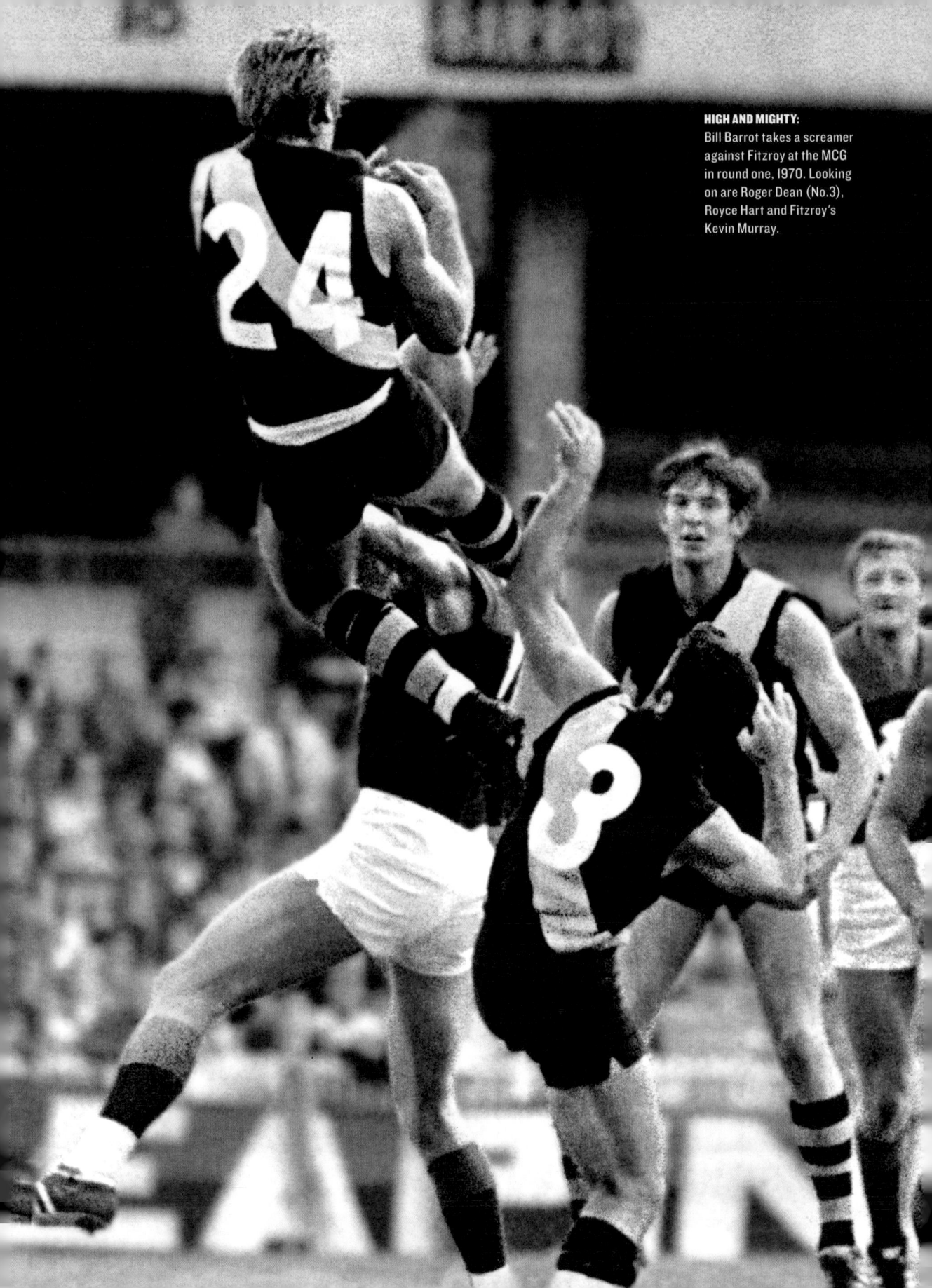

HIGH AND MIGHTY: Bill Barrot takes a screamer against Fitzroy at the MCG in round one, 1970. Looking on are Roger Dean (No.3), Royce Hart and Fitzroy's Kevin Murray.

Ruck
Michael Green
Games for Richmond: 146
(1966-71, 1973-75) Goals: 83

Michael Green was an outstanding finals player. His 1969 final series, when he beat Len Thompson and John Nicholls, is legendary.

He was a great mark, and very mobile for his size. He was an outstanding tap ruckman, and had soft hands and an impressive leap. His timing was perfect. I still maintain that his retirement at the end of 1971 in order to finish his law studies cost us the next year's Grand Final against Carlton.

When he came out of retirement we won the 1973 and '74 premierships and he was dominant in both Grand Finals. In his first game for Richmond in 1966, he played full-back against South Melbourne on Austin Robertson jnr. It turned out to be a very short stay in defence. Roger Dean played in the back pocket and constantly chipped in front of Robertson to take the mark because 'Greeny' had no idea.

And yet he was named in the back pocket in Richmond's Team of the Century. Obviously the selectors felt he was too good to leave out of the starting line-up. The first time I ever saw Michael was when he came down from Assumption College to play in the under-17s. He was tall and skinny. We then played together in the under-19s at Richmond. After moving into the ruck in the seniors he became a great big game player. Few players stood up better when the heat was on. He was a magnificent player and he played in four premiership teams.

Ruck-Rover
Bill Barrot
Games for Richmond: 120 (1961-70)
Goals: 91

Bill was a mercurial player with a massive kick. When he was firing no one could beat him and that's why I have put him on the ball. He played his career mostly in the role of a ruck-rover, running where he liked all over the field, even when named in the centre.

He had the ability to kick goals from full-forward and that's what he did in 1969 to help us make the finals. Against Carlton late in the season, he was moved to the goalsquare at half-time and he booted eight goals on Wes Lofts. Tom Hafey made the same move on several occasions during the 1967 and '69 finals to give the side a spark.

Bill was the first player in my knowledge to hit the weights. Back in our day, Tigerland didn't really have a gym; you had to go to a gymnasium yourself or do your weights at home. Bill was ahead of his time in terms of fitness. He was an Adonis, a real powerhouse.

Rover
Dale Weightman
Games for Richmond: 274 (1978-93)
Goals: 344

Dale, better known as 'Flea', was an incredible player for his size. He had magic hands and his handballing was on a par with the great Barry Cable. He had tremendous ability to change direction; his running swerve as he ran with the ball was one of the great sights in football.

Flea played 275 games and if it weren't for diabetes, achilles injuries and suspensions there is no doubt he would have played 300 games. He was very fiery and was reported 16 times. I admired him greatly because he was a target for opponents who would try to take him out of the game and often he retaliated.

He seemed born to be a rover but, strangely given his height, he was recruited to Richmond as a centre half-forward. He probably should have kicked more goals for the Tigers but he was so busy helping others to kick them.

Interchange
David Cloke
Games for Richmond: 219
(1974-82, 1990-91) Goals: 272

David is in my side because he was a mighty ruckman who had a tremendous knack when playing a kick behind the play. He could read the ball coming into defence as well as anyone.

KING OF THE JUNGLE: Royce Hart carries the 1974 premiership cup in the company of (from left) Barry Richardson, Daryl Cumming, Francis Bourke, Wayne Walsh and Gareth Andrews.

He was capable of dominating at centre half-forward and he also had dominant games at full-forward or in a forward pocket. In his first premiership, in 1974, he played as a tall, skinny half-forward flanker before developing into a monster of a man.

He had enormous endurance for a man of his size. He would always be one of the fastest when we did laps of the Tan Track at Melbourne's Royal Botanic Gardens. I was always impressed at his enormous ability to push his body.

He was very unselfish, and protective of smaller players. His weakness, of course, was his kicking. He forever worked on his action and his accuracy, but he remained an ungainly kick. David wasn't a knock 'em down type but he used his bulk to block opponents, and he was impossible to get around.

Interchange
Wayne Walsh
Games for Richmond: 88
(1968, 1972-75, 1977-78)
Goals: 30

Wayne Walsh failed in his first stint at Tigerland and so he went to South Melbourne. We had many great centre-line players so it was good to see him succeed at South Melbourne, where he made the Victorian team as a defender.

But then he had a falling out with South's legendary coach Norm Smith, so we were fortunate to get him back to Richmond. Wayne was a big-game player who had a thumping kick, and he starred in the 1973 and '74 final series as a wingman. He was cheeky and very confident. He'd have a go at opponents using his quick wit.

Interchange
Kevin Morris
Games for Richmond: 110 (1971-76)
Goals: 70

Kevin was a best-and-fairest winner and dual premiership player who could play as a half-forward flanker or across half-back and even as a ruck-rover. He was very strong, and a good mark and kick. He was always totally committed to his football and was a team-oriented player. His specialty was just getting things done and doing them properly. In that respect, his approach was similar to that of Francis Bourke.

Interchange
Bryan Wood
Games for Richmond: 209 (1972-82)
Goals: 85

In a team so blessed with centre-line players, I had to squeeze Bryan out of the starting 18 and on to the bench. He fitted Richmond's style brilliantly – a 185cm wingman who was quick, a good kick, covered a lot of ground and took strong marks.

He was Richmond captain for a season, in 1981, and he played in three premierships (1973, '74 and

'80). He also played in a flag team with Essendon, in 1985. I always found he had a great record playing against Keith Greig, who was later to be named in the AFL Team of the Century. Bryan was able to match him in great duels and the club was poorer when he left to become an Essendon player.

Emergency
Mark Lee
Games for Richmond: 233 (1977-91)
Goals: 94

'The General' was a ruckman who was amazingly athletic for his height. I couldn't get over how quick he was for a man who was 199cm.

His agility made him an outstanding player and his best football came when it mattered most, the 1980 finals series, when he destroyed everyone with his all-round brilliance.

His ruckwork was team-lifting stuff; he ran in at the centre bounce, leapt high and thumped the ball 25 metres. He was one of the few ruckman at that stage whose game included ground skills, strength, power, and leg-speed. He was as much a giant midfielder as he was a ruckman.

Mark was club captain, a best-and-fairest winner and an All-Australian, but injuries curtailed his strength towards the end of his career. He didn't have the sure hands of Michael Green, but his midfield skills set him apart.

Emergency
Barry Rowlings
Games for Richmond: 152 (1979-86)
Goals: 118

Barry was a premiership player with Hawthorn, in 1976, but the Hawks thought he was finished when he suffered a knee injury late in 1978. He grabbed his chance at Richmond with both hands. He won a best and fairest in his first season (1979), a premiership in 1980 and became captain in 1983. His killer left-foot was his defining trait. But he was a super competitor, and versatile. He played as a rover, ruck-rover, wing or centre.

CONVINCING WIN: Bruce Monteath hoists the 1980 premiership cup.

Emergency
Bruce Monteath
Games for Richmond: 118 (1975-80)
Goals: 198

Bruce was underrated. He was an excellent goalkicker who could play as a ruck-rover or a forward. He averaged nearly two goals a game in his six seasons at Tigerland.

His ability in front of goals was highlighted by the fact that he won a club goalkicking award despite not being a key forward; in 1978 he kicked 55 goals. He was captain of the 1980 premiership side but went into the game with a very bad ankle injury and was fortunate to be there. He was able to get himself just fit enough to pull through. He had mental toughness and determination.

He was a top-line, consistent player for Richmond with a touch of class.

PLAYING THE GAME

THE BEST OF MY ERA

I'm not sure if the era I played in was the best of all time, but a team made up from the best players of my era has champions across every line.

Anytime anyone is asked to select a best side of any description, it is difficult to fit in every great player. And if you played for 19 seasons, as I was fortunate enough to do, then there are really three different types of careers I needed to choose from.

Firstly, there were those such as Kevin Murray and Bob Skilton, who started in the 1950s, in both cases nearly a decade before my first game for Richmond in 1965. At the other end of the scale there were those such as Peter Daicos, Doug Hawkins and Tim Watson, who started towards the end of my career and were still going around a decade after my retirement in 1983. That being the case, the only fair criterion was to select players who played the bulk of their careers during my time as a player. It contains seven Brownlow medallists and between them, members of this team won 61 club best and fairest awards.

It starts with the back line, which is so attacking, with Ian Nankervis, David Dench and Trevor Barker – all rebounding players and well suited to the modern game. Geoff Southby and Peter Knights were thumping kicks and great in the air. Bruce Doull just beat everyone and never fumbled, always maintaining his extraordinary concentration.

The centerline would match any other combination the game has produced. Keith Greig, Peter Bedford and Robert Flower – what skill and flair!

The forward set-up is breathtaking and would be a nightmare to defend. The half-forward line contains Alex Jesaulenko and Malcolm Blight, two of the most mercurial players ever, lined up on either side of Bernie Quinlan. All three kicked 100 goals in a season.

Peter Hudson mesmerized everyone with his uncanny goalsense. Len Thompson and Garry Wilson, resting off the ball, would help form a lethal attack.

Simon Madden, Michael Tuck and Leigh Matthews - what a trio. They pick themselves. Madden was not only a great ruckman, but he also kicked more than 500 career goals. Tuck, the League's games record holder with 426 games would have won numerous best and fairest awards if not for his Hawthorn teammate Matthews – arguably the game's greatest player.

It's almost embarrassing to name Gary Dempsey, Wayne Schimmelbusch, Wayne Richardson and Barry Cable on the bench, given what impact players they are. Two greats of Carlton, David McKay and Robert Walls, together with Magpie spearhead Peter McKenna (squeezed out by Hudson) would be my emergencies.

But if you want to know how strong this side would be, consider some of those who were unlucky not to get in. Stan Alves (Melbourne and North Melbourne), John Murphy (Fitzroy, South Melbourne and North Melbourne), Graham Moss (Essendon), Greg Wells (Melbourne and Carlton) and Bruce Nankervis (Geelong) topped the list.

Kevin Bartlett's Best Team (1965-83)

COACH
Ron Barassi
CARLTON, NORTH MELBOURNE,
MELBOURNE, SYDNEY

RUCKS
Simon Madden
ESSENDON
Michael Tuck
HAWTHORN
Leigh Matthews
HAWTHORN

BACKS
Ian Nankervis	David Dench	Geoff Southby
GEELONG	NORTH MELBOURNE	CARLTON

HALF-BACKS
Bruce Doull	Peter Knights	Trevor Barker
CARLTON	HAWTHORN	ST KILDA

CENTRES
Keith Greig	Peter Bedford	Robert Flower
NORTH MELBOURNE	SOUTH MELBOURNE, CARLTON	MELBOURNE

HALF-FORWARDS
Alex Jesaulenko	Bernie Quinlan	Malcolm Blight
CARLTON	FOOTSCRAY, FITZROY	NORTH MELBOURNE

FORWARDS
Len Thompson	Peter Hudson	Garry Wilson
COLLINGWOOD, SOUTH MELBOURNE, FITZROY	HAWTHORN	FITZROY

INTERCHANGE
Gary Dempsey
FOOTSCRAY, NORTH MELBOURNE
Barry Cable
NORTH MELBOURNE
Wayne Schimmelbusch
NORTH MELBOURNE
Wayne Richardson
COLLINGWOOD

EMERGENCIES
David McKay
CARLTON
Robert Walls
CARLTON, FITZROY
Peter McKenna
COLLINGWOOD, CARLTON

KB
COACHING THE GAME

FAMILY CLUB: Michael (left) and Justin Pickering were fixtures of the Richmond side I coached between 1988 and 1991.

KB
COACHING THE GAME

COACHING MEMORIES

I accepted the opportunity to coach the club I loved without a moment's hesitation. It soon emerged I was in for a bumpy ride.

Early in 1987 I received a phone call from Richard Doggett, who was then general manager of the Tigers. He sounded me out on whether I would be interested in coaching the Tigers. And I said, 'You have Tony Jewell as the coach,' and he said, 'Tony has indicated he wants to move away from coaching.' I didn't feel comfortable talking to them about coaching the Tigers, because Tony had been a teammate of mine and coach of the 1980 premiership team.

BIG JOB: Tony Jewell's second stint as Richmond coach ended when I replaced him in late 1987.

IN WITH THE NEW: This photo was taken on the day I was announced as Richmond coach, in September 1987. The man I replaced, former teammate Tony Jewell, is smiling wryly at what I was getting myself into. Dusty O'Brien, a much-loved property steward for decades, witnesses another changing of the guard.

He was then in his second stint as Richmond coach after being sacked in 1981 and reinstated in 1986.

But Richard assured me that Tony had said to them that he wanted to give the coaching away. So I said, 'If that's the case, I will have a chat to you.'

I met with the committee and re-iterated that I didn't want to be going for a job that was already held by Tony, and even said, 'Who knows, the second half of the season the Tigers may play well and Tony may want to continue, so the club should be putting its efforts in to finishing off as well as they can.' As things turned out, they came back and said, 'Tony definitely wants to move on,' and they would offer me the job if I wanted to take it.

Coaching was something I was always keen to do so I accepted the job. I remember saying to them, 'There will be a lot of work required to get the Richmond Football Club up. The club will need far better players than we have.

Tony has already proved himself to be a premiership coach, so if the team is sitting on the bottom of the ladder, I thought, it would not be because of the coaching, but because the club has deficiencies in a lot of other areas. It soon became clear most of our problems were financial.

I took on the job because I loved the club dearly. I had knocked back two other coaching offers from Melbourne and Fitzroy in the past, but I just felt this immense loyalty to Richmond. If I were going to coach I would rather do it with the club I loved and had played my entire career.

I realised the club was in a sorry state when I didn't even really have an office. There was a players' room with a bit of carpet and some steps on it and a blackboard and I had a desk sitting in there.

When I first took over, I was the only full-time coach. Bruce Seymour was football operations manager, and he was tremendous. He was hard-working; nothing was too much for Bruce. But it seemed to me that Bruce was all we had in a support role.

The rooms themselves hadn't changed from when I was playing – the conditions were as bad as in 1965 when I played my first game. Bruce actually repainted the rooms himself during the Christmas break, and it was Bruce who re-laid the carpet. So you can see it was very unprofessional and under-resourced.

I had a good look at the gym before we started training. Half the weights were missing, there was a punching bag hook but no punching bag, there were fittings for speed balls but there were no speed balls and half the mechanics holding the speedballs were broken or gone. I remember buying four or five speed balls and putting them up myself.

We did have terrific support around the club. Phil Grant, for example, who he was running his own sporting business; out of the goodness of his heart he produced the mitts so you could hit the speedballs; he produced weights that were missing, boxing gloves and any little bits he could help out with. He was one of a number of terrific people with terrific hearts putting in to help the Richmond Football Club.

Michael Green was absolutely superb as chairman of selectors. He was fantastic with his wisdom. Frank Dimattina, a busy restaurateur, came down as

START OF SOMETHING: I was full of optimism when this photo was taken just after my appointment as Richmond coach in September 1987.

BRAINS TRUST: (Clockwise from bottom left) Lloyd Brown (statistics), Barry Rowlings (assistant coach), Eric Leech (committeeman), Mike Green (chairman of selectors), Emmett Dunne (reserves coach), me, George McHutchison (coach's assistant) and Bill Meaklim (statistics) weigh up our prospects during a pre-season match at VFL Park on January 30, 1988.

team manager; somehow he found time out from his restaurant business, he just wanted to help the club. He used to bring down pizzas every Thursday night to feed an entire football team at no cost. Paul Callery is a great mate of mine; he came down and he was our runner and fitness adviser and was absolutely fantastic.

Paul was always getting reported and fined for refusing to leave the ground after relaying a message. But let me tell you this: Paul Callery was one of the best things that ever happened to the Richmond Football Club. He not only did all the Phys Ed work for a pittance; he was the club runner and a selector for one year. His enthusiasm for the club, his spirit and friendship were second to none. He had ability to bring people together. He was like

a sports psychologist at the time, and these does he has a PhD.

Paul was one of those great people you want around. Good people breed good people. Paul regularly anticipated what I was going to say. He was a player himself and got verbal when he was runner if he saw anything untoward. As a result he was constantly getting fined. Which was a bit of a worry for us, because we had no money to pay the fines!

Ken Stonehouse, a selector, was one of a bunch of blokes who gave so much to the club during the years I was coach. So did Emmett Dunne, who was my assistant coach and coach of the reserves. I didn't know the club was in great debt until several months after I had accepted the job. It came as a

FAMILIAR FIST: I acknowledge the fans after defeating St Kilda at the MCG in round 12, 1990.

WIN IN THE WET: Brian Leys (left), Andy Goodwin, Michael Mitchell and Allister Scott celebrate after defeating Essendon at Windy Hill in round 17, 1991. At left are clippings from my first official game as coach.

bit of a surprise to me before the annual general meeting at the Richmond Social Club.

We finished training and the board asked me to their meeting. They then told me they were going to make an announcement that the club was $1.5 million in debt, at that time an enormous sum of money. That was disappointing. Immediately we knew we weren't going to be in a position to and buy any players to help the club fast-track itself from the bottom of the ladder.

You couldn't buy players without money. I can remember going across with Bruce Seymour to South Australia to draft a few players, and staying with friends because the club didn't have money to put you in a hotel. In one of the earlier days, it was so wet, the ground was in such bad condition, that we decided to train indoors at the Royal Park

Netball Centre. Barry Rowlings, another fantastic person and a 1980 Premiership teammate, was doing the skills work and he ran around all day trying to find someone from the club to give him $50 to hire the courts.

It sounds ridiculous, but if you've got no money, you've got no money. I can still recall Barry saying, 'I can't find anybody.' Anyway, he got $50 from someone and I can remember, while training was taking place indoors, Barry coming up to me, ashen-faced. I said, 'What's wrong?' and he said, 'You won't believe what's happened.' I thought, 'Don't tell me I've lost one of the young kids.' And he said, 'Someone has just broken a window.' I said, 'Well, what can we do about that?'

He said, 'How are we going to pay for it?'

We went on a training camp up near Moe. We could take only a certain number of players because we couldn't afford to take the whole group. The idea was that half would stay back in Melbourne and the other half would go and we would make up some reason why they all couldn't go.

In the end I said, 'We can't do that, that's ridiculous.' So we all went on the training camp and I spent about $300 hiring some motivational sporting films. It was a difficult time for coaching staff and the board as well, because they had the responsibility of not only trying to keep the club afloat but keeping it viable.

We had some early picks in the mid-season draft and could have picked up players like Derek Kickett from Essendon and Tim Pekin from Fitzroy. But we were told under no circumstances could we draft those players because we just didn't have any money to pay what they wanted. So we could only stick with the policy of drafting young kids out of school – sometimes still going to school – and maybe drafting someone from the country who hadn't made it before.

Russell Morris, who grew up loving the Tigers and was a terrific player with Hawthorn, wanted to come to Richmond, but we were offering only half as much money as he had been offered by St Kilda – and St Kilda wasn't setting the world on fire in those days.

I was desperate to get some experience, strength and agility into the team, so much so that I even rang Geoff Raines after he finished with the Brisbane Bears at the end of 1989 to come back and play. But Geoff was setting himself up in business in Brisbane and said it was not feasible to make the move.

David Cloke was coming to the end of his time as a player at Collingwood but to me he was still good enough to get a game at Richmond.

He would walk into our side and be great for our young kids because he was a very, very hard trainer, a fabulous player and former captain of the club. So I rang David and said, 'I know you're coming to the end of your career but I need some help. I need someone in the club who can lead, someone with a bit of size and credibility. Would you be interested?'

STERN: I borrowed a bit from Tom Hafey in my time as coach.

HAPPY ENDING: David Cloke is chaired off by Jeff Hogg (left), Brian Leys and Scott Turner after his last game, the round-24 defeat of Carlton in 1991. David kicked eight that day. The match was at the MCG during the period when the southern stand was under construction.

And he said, 'Yeah, I would be interested. I think I still can play.' I said, 'We've got one problem, David, we haven't got any money at all so we can't offer you any big contracts, any signing-on fees, you'll have to come back just out of the goodness of your heart, virtually.' And David said, 'Look, football has been good to me. I have done well, I'll just play for match payments.' And that's what he did.

David had two fantastic seasons (1990–91) with us. He retired after the first season and then I talked him into coming back again and it was just great.

We may not have had too many happy days when I was coach of the Tigers but my last game, even though it was sad for me, probably was still a highlight when David – also in his last game – kicked eight goals against Carlton.

My most disappointing loss as Richmond coach was against Hawthorn at Waverley Park in round 18, 1991. In the preceding years, Hawthorn had belted us by as many goals as they liked, with Jason Dunstall and Dermott Brereton starring. But in 1991, after we had some bigger and stronger kids in the side, we had Hawthorn beaten with five minutes left.

I placed Jeff Hogg at full-back that day and he played a tremendous game, keeping Dunstall to only two goals. Then Dunstall kicked his third in the dying moments to enable Hawthorn to beat us by six points. The Hawks had humiliated us early in the year by 57 points and the previous year by 91 points. Here was our chance to get one back and we just failed.

Hawthorn was behind one of the most disappointing days on a football field I have ever seen. It was round 15, 1989. We were third last on the ladder and Hawthorn was on top.

Peter Czerkaski was playing for us that day. The previous week, Peter had tagged Sydney's Barry Mitchell and kept him to 10 possessions.

Now Peter was as fair as they come, he didn't have a bad bone in his body. He was fit and a great sprinter and he thwarted Mitchell with no

NARROW MISS: Richmond's Brian Leys prepares to pounce in round 18, 1991, my biggest letdown as coach. We were in front until late.

man-handling at all. He just played close and got his body in the way.

Against Hawthorn, we put Peter on Gary Buckenara. And very early in the first quarter, Peter was knocked out behind play. He hadn't even touched the ball. If you check his stats for the game, the only figure is "0".

Not long after the incident I turned to the Hawthorn coach's box, which was next to me, and yelled expletives at the coaching panel led by Allan Jeans. 'You f****** call yourself a f****** Family club!' I screamed, pounding on the window.

A little bit later on, Brereton ran through Des Ryan off the ball so I was very irate. After the game, I called every Hawthorn player a thug and I claimed that Hawthorn was bending the rules and getting away with it because they were the best side in the competition. Everyone was turning a blind eye to Hawthorn's rough play.

The League charged me with abusing the umpires in my press conference. I had to appear before league

WHOLE HOGG: Jeff Hogg (left) and David Cloke soak up the congratulations after Hogg's 10 goals against Collingwood in round 8, 1991.

administrator and former Richmond secretary-manager Alan Schwab at League headquarters for a please explain and I just told him the truth as I saw it. 'Blokes are being knocked out cold and being run through and no one is doing anything about it, yet I stand here before you with a please explain because of something I said. This place is a joke.'

I was fined a couple of thousand dollars. The Richmond cheer squad, led by David Norman, took the hat around and raised the money to pay for the fine. Buckenara had been reported for striking Czerkaski and Hawthorn got him off at the tribunal with some cock-and-bull story that he turned to run back and they collided. Everyone at Richmond knew the truth.

Gary is one of the nicest people you could ever meet and it was completely out of character for him. I don't know what went through his mind that day. There *were* good times. In my first year, 1988, we played reigning premiers Carlton in a night match in Round 12. We were given no chance of winning because we were last and Carlton was in second place.

We were just a bunch of kids – the average age that night was 23 years. Chris Pym was playing his fifth game for us and he kicked three goals in the last quarter to shoot the Tigers to victory. Chris didn't have a long career but he covered himself in glory that night.

Peter Wilson played a great game across half-flank. At the end of the game he did a cartwheel, which no one had seen on a League football ground before.

One of my most rewarding victories as coach was when the Tigers defeated Geelong, the previous year's runner-up, at Geelong in round 7, 1990. We as a club were struggling to stay afloat and everyone expected the Cats to annihilate us. We had won only one game, against Fitzroy in Round 5, while Geelong had won their previous four games.

Before the match, all the football writers tipped Geelong to slaughter us. Bill Jacobs on 3AW said we were odds of a million to one to win.

My line before the match was that the only person in Australia who has tipped us to win was my old teammate Michael Roach, who was writing for *Inside Football*, and even he was dodgy about tipping us. It was a day when Benny Gale showed he was going to be a great player for us.

He was 21 years old and very raw. Unfortunately, in his early games he didn't kick very straight, but showed us he was a strong mark. He became a focal point for us in this game. David Cloke and Mark Lee, aged 35 and 31 respectively, changed off the interchange bench at 10-minute intervals to keep the pressure on Geelong.

Andy Goodwin was playing his first game at full-back. He was a rough and tough and far from highly skilled, but he had tremendous enthusiasm and, again because we lacked size and height, we played him in the last line of defence at full-back.

We alternated Des and Stephen Ryan from the wing to opposite forward pockets with Michael Mitchell, and they kicked six goals between them.

Geelong finished up kicking 9.28. We kicked 13.18 and won by 14 points.

That match was on the Mothers' Day weekend. The following year, we had another a successful day on Mothers' Day. In 1991, we defeated Collingwood at the MCG by 57 points. Jeff Hogg kicked 10.1.

The Save Our Skins campaign was launched on August 15, 1990. Three weeks later, we played Sydney at the SCG, and every Tigers player and coach was asked to donate their wage for the day to the Save our Skins rally.

That, of course, was the famous game in which Michael Mitchell ran from half-back to the forward line to kick the goal of the year. The next day, we all huddled in the gymnasium at the club. While watching a replay of the match, we kept rewinding the tape at that magic moment.

Another great memory was beating Kevin Sheedy's Bombers at Windy Hill in Round 17, 1991. It was the last time the two great clubs met at that ground.

Essendon, like Hawthorn, was accustomed to destroying us. The previous year, in 1990, the Bombers defeated us by 78 and 79 points in our two games. Richmond had not won at Windy Hill since 1983, my last year as a player.

So we took some strong bodies out to Windy Hill for the match in wet, windy and cold conditions. Players like Brian Leys, Des Ryan, Andrew Underwood and Scott Turner created opened paths for their teammates and played their hearts out in a slogfest.

It was very satisfying, as a coach, to see the players apply themselves so whole-heartedly. It would have been easier to throw in the towel on such a difficult day, but they didn't. I felt very proud that day to be coach.

HANDS ON: Peter Wilson (left) and Jeff Hogg in action in a night match against Carlton.

Now, as a member of the Laws of the Game committee, I often refer back to another match I was coaching: round 7, 1989, against West Coast at Waverley Park.

Michael Pickering was ostensibly chasing a player on the outer side of the ground; really, he was sheep-dogging the player with the ball because he was too far away to tackle. That is, he was trying to stop the Eagles player from cutting back into play. Geoff Miles from West Coast came out of nowhere mowed down Pickering and Michael was KO'd.

Our club doctor and trainer had to put a tube down Michael's throat to assist his breathing. He was in a very serious state. Michael was one of the fairest and bravest players I had ever meet.

That's why, as a member of the Laws of Game Committee, I am a strong advocate of stamping out the practice of taking out players who are no threat to the player with the ball.

In 2010, the Law was changed to protect the player chasing. If he is knocked out because someone decides to run through him, then that aggressor is deemed responsible and is subject to assessment by the match review panel.

GOING BUST: The media covered Richmond's plight extensively.

Save Our Skins

One of the most important periods during my four years as Richmond coach was the 'Save Our Skins' campaign in October 1990, which raised $1 million and saved the club from being shut down.

Thinking back, I believe my actions may have been a key reason for the campaign starting.

I remember talking to the board about needing new players and whether the club had a recruiting budget, only to be told there was no money for recruiting.

Come the 1990 mid-season draft, we were unable to pick up experienced players because we had no money to pay them. We really were only able to recruit young boys, only 16 or 17, who were still at school and eager to play League football.

One day, I just got jack of it.

I remember saying to Doug Vickers, who was then my Football Operations Manager, 'I can't take this anymore. Give me a list of all the players who could be listed in the mid-season draft and I am just going to pick the best credentialled person, even though we won't be able to afford him".

So Doug got me the list. We painstakingly appraised each name and finally decided on South Australian Andrew Payze, who clearly had the best reputation of the players in that draft.

Payze had already finished runner-up in the 1986 Magarey Medal and had been drafted to Essendon. But he never played senior football at Windy Hill. He remained in Adelaide and played for his state in the 1988 Bicentennial Carnival.

As a previous draftee, he was eligible for the draft even though he hadn't nominated, so I declared to Doug that irrespective of what might happen, we were going to take Payze with our first mid-season pick.

Before the draft I went to Adelaide and I met up with Andrew and his wife. He was a lovely guy, and I asked him, 'What are the chances of you coming to play with Richmond if I draft you?' His response was, 'Very little chance, KB. I'm in the retention fund.' The South Australian National

CROWE CALL: As president, Neville Crowe did a wonderful job of rallying the Tigers towards eradicating the club's debt.

EVERY PENNY COUNTS: Volunteers of all ages helped to raise $1 million to keep the club alive.

Football League had created a fund aimed at keeping their best players in the state so that they would be available to play for an Adelaide-based AFL team if one was to be created. It meant that many of the best SA players were off limits. They were being paid good money not to move across to Melbourne.

So I flew back to Melbourne knowing there was no chance that Andrew Payze was going to play for the Richmond Football Club.

Still, I drafted him.

I went to a Richmond board meeting soon afterwards and said, 'Andrew Payze is the major player I wanted for this club. He is a club captain, a leader, and a strong player. But we have no money to bring him across, which is sad, because he told me he is very keen to play for Richmond.'

Granted, I was telling fibs to the board, but I wanted to put pressure on the club, to show them how not being able to recruit players was going to kill the club.

I looked across at each of the board members and said, 'If we are in a position where we can't even get Andrew Payze across to Tigerland, well, we might as well pack up the joint. What are we doing? Why are we even here?''

A week or so afterwards, our chairman Neville Crowe announced to the media that the club was broke and needed to raise $1 million or go out of business. With that, the Save Our Skins campaign was born.

We never got Payze over to Tigerland. He ended up playing for Adelaide in its maiden AFL season in 1991 before returning to the SANFL, where he ended up playing 308 games for West Torrens and Woodville-West Torrens.

He's now a board member of the Crows. But we did raise the money required to keep the Richmond Football Club in existence.

A lot of officials and volunteers worked very hard during that time, particularly Crowe, who was the figurehead of the club and the face of the campaign.

GALVANISING EXPERIENCE: Richmond cheer-squad leader David Norman rallies the Tiger hordes.

We all rattled tins, organised the Save our Skins rally, travelled around the country visiting supporter groups, sold sausages in the street, and visited shopping centres – all to raise money.

Supporters from other clubs were fantastic. I had people come up hand over their donations. They would say, 'I barrack for Carlton but we can't have Richmond dying.'

The support from fans of other clubs really touched me. It showed me what football really meant to them, and how inter-club rivalries were still important for them.

Thinking back, I don't know how much money we raised. Even though I was the coach and I kept asking how the fundraising was going, I was never told how much we finally raised. It could have been exactly $1 million or perhaps double that.

I just know it was enough to keep the Tigers alive.

The Old-Fashioned Way

No computers here. It was old-school coaching in 1988, with a clipboard and satchel. Statistics were handwritten, and the club's footage of each game was shot by a single camera high up in the Ponsford Stand. Sponsorship, too, was at a minimum – a small Drink Drive logo the sole advertisement on the coaching jacket. Simply put – the game was yet to become commercialised.

Drink, drive, bloody idiot.

KB
COACHING THE GAME

SACKED AS COACH

My time as coach came to an abrupt and disappointing end in 1991. Angry and hurt, I stayed away from Richmond for a considerable period of time.

I was at home, peeling potatoes a few days after round 22, 1991, when I got the sack. My wife had gone out and had left specific instructions to prepare a roast for that night when Neville Crowe and Cameron Schwab knocked on the door.

I let them in and they told me pretty quickly that they were going to replace me with Allan Jeans in a couple of hours' time at a media conference. I was pretty angry as you would expect, so there was no point continuing any further discussions with them. I ordered them out. They had been there for no more than five minutes.

Amazingly, Tommy Hafey turned up only a few minutes after that. There had been a lot of things in the media at that time and about my position as coach (not that anyone from the club had spoken to me about it) and he dropped by to see how I was going.

I told Tommy it hadn't been a good day and that I'd been sacked as coach, so he came in. We sat down had a cup of tea, and we just chatted about life in general, footy and the way things happen. Tommy was very disappointed for me, because he knew what the club was going through and what we had to work with.

The press turned up not long after. Bruce Matthews from the *Herald Sun*, who I knew very well, was the first to arrive.

I told him I wanted to take a deep breath and wasn't going to make any comments to him or to any other journalist. 'Narra' as he is known, stayed

LAST TIME: I walk on to the MCG for my final game as Richmond coach. It's round 24, 1991, against Carlton. David Cloke kicked eight goals and the Tigers won, but it couldn't save me. At left is a newspaper poster from 1991 announcing my sacking.

FOUR POINTS IN THE BAG: Flanked by president Neville Crowe (obscured), committeeman Eric Leech (left) and Emmett Dunne (selector), I head towards the dressing rooms after a win at the MCG in 1991.

for a chat and a cup of tea as well. By that stage, the place was crawling with reporters, some managing to make it up onto a balcony and tapping on windows. But I kept my counsel.

I got a lot of phone calls from the players as well over the following days, which was terrific and I then sat down and wrote a little note to every player at the club, thanking them for their support and their efforts towards the club and me.

Thinking back, there were a lot of really good people on the Richmond board at that time. I liked virtually all of them and they seemed to be doing their best and trying really hard for the club.

My disappointment with them was they realised themselves how difficult it was at that time, and that I was trying to keep spirits high and keep the playing list afloat, but I believed they took the easy way out.

They should have understood how tough the battle was. And so that's why I was disappointed with the board. I don't know what forces made them buckle at the knees but they knew better than anyone how tough it was to coach the club in such dire straits.

One of the reasons I stayed away from the club was that I felt that Richmond, as a club had lost its soul and it got blurred into thinking that a good strong decision was to sack the coach.

It was this type of thinking that had harmed the club for too long. Even back in the days of Tommy Hafey it was made it obvious to him that he was out of favour and that he had to resign.

Then Barry Richardson took over and made the finals in one of his two years and then he too got the sack, which should never have happened.

Then Tony Jewell came in and coached the club for three years and won the premiership and then was sacked 12 months later. There was no way known that should have happened. Then Francis Bourke came in and coached the club to a Grand Final and got the sack a year later.

Then things got really farcical with Mike Patterson sacked after one season, and then Paul

FIRST CALL: Coterie members got to hear the side on a Thursday night at Punt Road.

Sproule the same. By then Barry Richardson was president and he resigned after one season after having given Sproule his word that he would remain as coach.

It's as if Richmond had this ongoing view that making tough decisions was sacking coaches. And when I fell foul of that, I thought to myself, 'You know what, I'm going to give the club a miss.'

I came to the conclusion that the club didn't have any real respect for its people. If they sacked me without at least the opportunity to meet to discuss where the club was at and what its strengths and weaknesses were after my four years as coach, then the ethos of the club had fundamentally changed and I no longer wanted to be part of it.

It was a silent protest. I wanted to show that the club that it could no longer treat people as it had done and that if it wanted to dispense of its coaches

DARK DAY: Brian Leys (left), Stephen James, Michael Pickering and Justin Pickering lament after a big loss at Waverley Park in 1989.

in the future in a similar fashion, then there might be consequences. By replacing me with Allan Jeans it was like saying, 'Kevin's the fault, we are not winning any games because of him' and so they took the easy way out and brushed over how tough things were for everybody at the club.

In hindsight, I shouldn't have been surprised. It was yet another example of what Richmond had become, a club that was content to eat its own. And I decided not to be associated with that type of club for the foreseeable future.

To add a bizarre twist to all the sackings, the club would invariably invite all the sacked coaches back to the club for dinner the following year and pretend that nothing had happened.

It was as if it was trying to wash its hands of it all. Somehow, Richmond celebrated sacking its coaches thinking it was tough and strong administration. In actual fact, it was the opposite. It was unprofessional, non-supportive and lacking of vision.

In the time I was away, I was approached by a number of people to do things at the club. I was approached to be on the board, I was approached to try and oust somebody, I was approached to join a group to challenge the board and was approached to support people running for the board.

Every time someone approached me I dismissed the call out of hand. I didn't want to be seen as a person who was trying to get back at people, or run people out of office; I decided that I wanted to make a clean break.

When I walked away, I didn't know whether it would be five, 10 or 15 years, but at some stage I would come back.

I thought I had well and truly made a point about the way I had been treated. I felt very strongly that, after 26 years at the club (1965–91), I deserved the courtesy of sitting down with officials and going over what had been a pretty tough period for everyone.

They appointed Allan Jeans in my place, and I only point this out to prove that the real issue with the club wasn't the coach but money. Jeans won only five games in 1992, two less than the previous year under my coaching. In 1993 they appointed John Northey and he only won four games.

These were Grand Final coaches and they found the same difficulties I had put up with, including having to develop young kids who were so small and frail that it was almost unfair to put them on to the same ground as the strong men of Geelong, West Coast, Carlton and Essendon.

I had one say in the press, not long after I walked away, and then I shut up shop, choosing not to criticise any individual at the club.

I did go to selected events. Tom Hafey has been a great inspiration to me and a great friend of the family. He is the man behind the Tommy Hafey Club and I thought on a couple of occasions that I would go. Sometimes I hadn't been able to because things have been on. But I thought in 2007 I would go.

I thought to celebrate my 60th birthday I would go to a Tommy Hafey Club function. The theme was the rivalry between Richmond and Carlton and I thought those clashes had always been very dear to me.

When I played, that was the biggest game of all. My last game as coach was against Carlton. So I thought that was a nice mix, turning 60, attending a Tommy Hafey Club function and celebrating a great rivalry with Carlton.

And Tom's first game as coach was against Carlton and I sat beside him as the 19th man, and on this afternoon, at the function, I sat beside him, too.

ONE OFF: I gave my only interview after my dismissal at Richmond to the *Herald Sun*.

Early last decade, I was granted Immortal status by the Richmond Football Club. I wasn't there on the night, because I was still on my self-imposed ban.

Looking back, my stance went on for too long. I think I made my point that I was disappointed with the way the club had acted. My son represented me on the Immortal night but, looking back, I should have been there on the night to accept the accolade.

KB
WATCHING THE GAME

ROVER AT LARGE: After finishing my playing career, I took a slot on *World of Sport* and my career as a broadcaster developed from there.

KB
WATCHING THE GAME

RETURNING TO TIGERLAND

It took a series of events to bring me back to Richmond, beginning with the realisation that none of us were getting any younger. I'm glad the ice was broken.

My return to Tigerland after my self-imposed 16-year exile came about after an unexpected meeting with an unlikely figure, Neville Crowe. Every year since my sacking as Tigers coach in 1991 I had attended the Richmond premiership players' reunion, which was put on by former president Ian Wilson just before the Grand Final.

OUT OF STEP: The scoop on my exit (left); a 1992 membership card, showing that my family went to one game for the season, against Melbourne at the MCG in round four.

It is a private gathering attended only by those who have played in a Richmond premiership team. No media. No wives. No girlfriends. Only those who have held a Richmond premiership cup aloft are allowed. In the past, players from the 1943 premiership team, such as Max Oppy and Arthur Barr-Kemp, have attended. The men who broke the drought in 1967 and then backed it up in '69 would be there. Members of 1973 and '74 back-to-back premierships, like Stephen Rae, would always attend, as would the guys from 1980, our last premiership side.

Just before the 2006 reunion, Ian Wilson asked me to get up and tell a few stories about those in the room. It was the first such function that Neville had attended because, technically, he didn't meet the criteria of a premiership player. He was accompanying Alan 'Bull' Richardson, who was in poor health at the time.

Neville had unfairly missed the 1967 Grand Final after being found guilty of striking Carlton's John Nicholls in the second semi-final, even though his attempted slap never made contact. At the time of his report and subsequent suspension, everyone at the club was so disappointed for him; to this day, we still believe an injustice occurred. So during the night of this reunion, the time came for me to stand

THE ENTRANCE: I return to Richmond for the launch of Rhett's history of the Tigers' first century. Behind me are Denise, Breanna and Rhett.

TESTING TALK: I speak to the media about my return to the Tigers after staying away from the club for 16 years; the launch of Rhett's book, with Francis Bourke (left) and Neville Crowe.

up and speak about each player. I began talking about the impact they had had on the club and the memories I had of them.

As I made my way around the room, Neville began to realise I was telling stories about each player. He thought to himself, 'Shit, what is going on here?'

When I got to Neville, I spoke very positively – from the heart, as I always have – about his contribution to the club, how he kept the spirits up at the club when the club was down, how he was the champion club ruckman of his time, the winner of three best-and-fairests, and a Victorian player. I made no comment about our disagreement at the end of my coaching career, because I greatly admire what he did for Richmond as a player, as a captain, and as the figurehead of the Save Our Skins campaign. He was also the captain when I began to play senior football in 1965.

After that I told stories about the other players before sitting back down at my table. That's when Neville approached me. He seemed a bit meek at first, and he thanked me for my kind words. My response? 'Neville,' I said, 'where's your moustache gone?'

Neville and I got on very well during my coaching tenure for all but the last few months. For 16 years since my coaching tenure we had not said a word to each other. As I was speaking to Neville, I realised that time was marching on. I was taken aback at how much he and others in the room had aged.

So I looked around the room a bit more and the realisation hit me that I was getting older as well, that I would be turning 60 in the coming months.

It was at that moment that I started to put things into perspective. To this day, I have never spoken to Neville about the circumstances surrounding my sacking. He and I have never broached the subject.

Around the time of the fateful premiership reunion, in late 2006, Tom Hafey was telling me about the Tommy Hafey Club and the tireless work of former players Mike Perry and Bruce Smith, in particular, in shaping it into a major fundraiser for the club.

After a time I came to understand his subtle reminders about how great the reunion events were. My wife, Denise, was also in my ear, telling me it was time to let go. I had made my point and it was time to move on.

Not long after that, Bruce Smith told me of an upcoming Tommy Hafey Club function focusing on the Richmond-Carlton rivalry, which to me was *the* rivalry of the late 1960s, the '70s into the early '80s. The function would be a celebration of a truly wonderful era. I told Bruce Smith that I would attend; it would be my first since my sacking as coach. But I stressed that he couldn't tell anyone because I didn't want any fuss. I just wanted to turn up and go to the function and support the Tommy Hafey Club. Only Bruce and my immediate family knew I was to attend. I told Bruce to keep a spot at the front table for me.

CENTURY-MAKERS: Francis Bourke (left), me, Tom Hafey, Ian Wilson, Michael Roach, Royce Hart, Michael Mitchell and Neville Crowe line up before the Tigers' centenary match, against Carlton in round 14, 2008. The Tigers wore historic black and yellow stripes for the match.

I remember I drove to the wrong hotel before arriving at the correct venue at 12.20pm. I just walked through all the tables towards the front table, where I ended up sitting between Francis Bourke and Tommy Hafey. Francis turned to me and said, 'Hello Kevin,' in his usual understated manner.

During the event many people came up and welcomed me back. It was a thrill to see some of the old supporters, officials and players, and since then I have been to other Richmond functions. I may have stayed away too long and I put my hand up for that because I can be stubborn at times.

During that time, I made an absolute priority of never getting involved in the politics of the club and never criticising anyone individually. As a commentator I spoke about Richmond as I would any other club. Even though I was away 16 years, I wasn't bitter. Some people say I was, but there was no bitterness. I never thought about it from the day I left. It was never on my mind. I just went on with my life and followed the Tigers as a supporter. I always attended our premiership reunions and apart from that I kept away.

A lot of people tried to get me back to the club. Coaches John Northey, Robert Walls, Jeff Gieschen and Danny Frawley all asked at one time or another if I could make an appearance, and I did do a video for Danny Frawley when he was getting some past players to talk about the passion and spirit at Tigerland in the 1960s and '70s. Media outlets would offer me money to come on their shows and talk about my sacking, and I was even offered money to attend a club function, accept an award and then leave. Presidents Leon Daphne and Clinton Casey had several discussions to see whether I could get involved again, but I politely declined all offers.

I always felt that by making a stand, it was sending a strong message to that board – or any board – that you should treat people with respect.

I kept thinking that one day other former Tiger champions such as Wayne Campbell, Matthew Knights or Tony Free might coach, and if they fell out with the club the board might think more carefully about making a change. They might say, 'Hang on, let's handle this appropriately, because we did this once to KB and he never came back.'

I always felt that if they had mistreated someone like me who had been there for 26 years, then heaven help the next person who comes along.

KB
WATCHING THE GAME

A LEGEND AND AN IMMORTAL

My good fortune in being honoured by the custodians of Australian football and by my club has prompted much reflection, then and now, with pride and with regret.

My selection as an AFL Legend is the greatest honour ever bestowed on me. It was such a wonderful night. It was lovely to have my whole family there, as well as my sons-in-law and Denise's mother, Laura, to share the moment. It was an enormous honour to be recognised by the panel.

As a kid, I barracked for the Bulldogs and Ted Whitten was a hero to me. Ron Barassi was a hero to everyone. And here I was being inducted into this elite group beside them.

I could never have ever guessed when I was a kid growing up or even during my playing days that I would be recognised for having had such an impact on the game.

The fact that I may have given people a lot of enjoyment along the way, or maybe had an effect on some who had followed the game or had loved the game as much as I do, is a very humbling experience.

It was a great night on which to reflect. As I stood on the stage I thought back to the fact that I was there in the initial induction of members, in 1996, alongside my great teammates in Royce Hart and Francis Bourke.

Memories came flooding back while I was on the stage. My dear Mum and Dad supported me all the way through my junior career.

While Dad worked, Mum would take time off work to watch me play for the tech school or the state school. Every Saturday morning Mum and Dad drove me to the under-17s and under-19s matches for Richmond.

NEW STATUS: Recognition (above) of my inauguration as a Legend in 2000; (left) my invitation as a Legend to the 2006 function to welcome in new Legends.

TOP HONOURS: I was thrilled to be an inaugural inductee into the AFL Hall of Fame in 1996 and named as a Hall of Fame Legend in 2000.

BIG NIGHT: My family (clockwise from bottom left) Breanna, Sharna, Denise, Cara and Rhett were with me the night I was named a Legend.

I thought back to kicking the football in the park and running around with my mates. I thought about the people who were a big part of my life: close family friends and teammates with whom I came up through the ranks. Some made it, some didn't, but they all were a part of my journey.

Then I remembered Bill Boromeo, my first coach and mentor; Lyall Johnson, the trainer at Richmond who looked after me for all my 403 games; and the coaches, from Len Smith, to Jack Titus, to Tom Hafey, Barry Richardson, Tony Jewell and so on.

And I looked back and realised I was being honoured for something they were all a part of. Without them I wouldn't have been there.

So many things were flowing through my mind as I tried to decipher how I got there.

I remember that after my speech I was asked to place my hands in wet cement. There was an idea to get the handprints of all the living Legends for exhibition when a Hall of Fame was created.

I have no idea what happened to those cement blocks.

I was very thrilled with the honour of becoming a Richmond Immortal. At that time I was estranged from the club because of my sacking as coach. In looking back I was too stubborn and I should have been there on the night, because the club had bestowed on me their highest individual honour.

Instead I sent my son on my behalf. At the time it was the most comfortable decision for me. But in hindsight it was a poor decision and a wrong decision and I should have shown more respect for the club. I should have been more gracious and I should have been there on the night.

I was glad I was represented by my family but on reflection I should have put differences aside so that the evening could be embraced.

Club officials contacted me several times to try to convince me to come. Being stubborn, I still rejected the invitations. I thank those officials for their persistence and I sincerely apologise for not accepting the invitation to that night.

I put my hand up and admit I got it wrong.

TOP TIGERS: Francis Bourke (left), Dick Clay, Royce Hart, Kevin Sheedy, Rhett (in my place, wearing my 403rd-game guernsey) and Roger Dean at the inaugural Richmond Hall of Fame presentation. At right is my plaque. Below is Clinton Casey's suggestion that I return to accept my award.

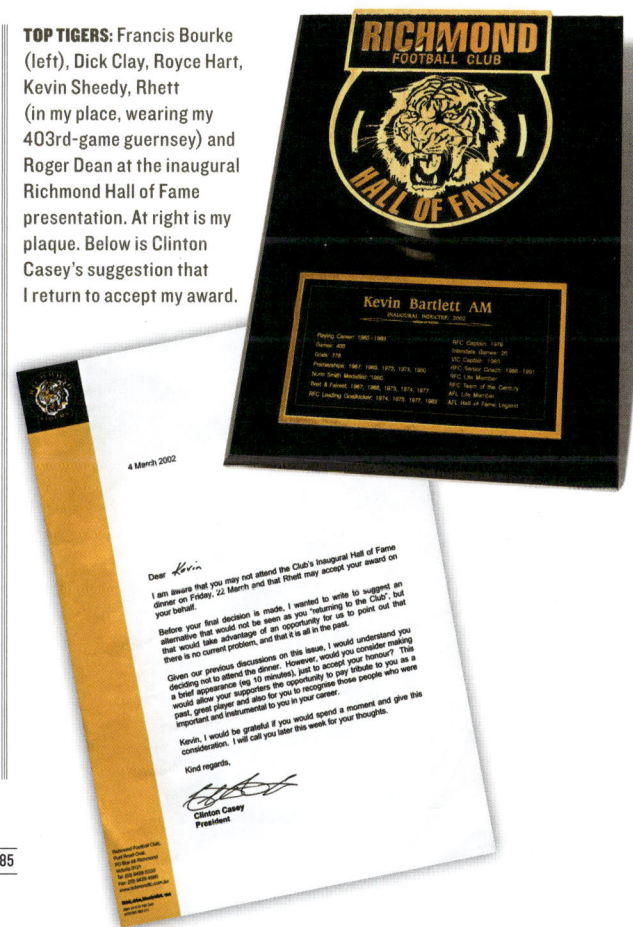

TRAIL OF BLOOD: My experiences as a player and coach led to my belief that every measure must be taken to protect players' heads. This area of concern became a priority for the AFL's Laws of the Game Committee.

WATCHING THE GAME

BENDING AND CHANGING THE RULES

Many would regard my presence on the Laws of the Game Committee with suspicion, given my opposition to a rule change in the 1970s, but I've enjoyed my role as a keeper of the code.

It is a little ironic that I am on the AFL Laws of the Game Committee, because back in my playing days, I was the main reason for a significant rule change. When I was in possession, I would bounce the ball just as my opponent was about to tackle me. Then I would throw my hands up to indicate to the umpire that I was being tackled while not in possession.

The umpire would penalise the tackler for 'holding the man'. I did this week in and week out. Players like Darrel Baldock of St Kilda and John Birt of Essendon occasionally did it, but not as much as me! It was a loophole that I utilised until late in 1972 when the biggest name in football, Ron Barassi, ratted me out.

Ron was writing a column in *The Sun* called "Column 31". In the column, he was very critical of those of us who were getting away with bouncing the ball before being tackled. He must have struck a nerve because, almost immediately, the rule was changed.

From then on, if you bounced the ball you were deemed to be still in possession, because the ball logically would be bouncing back towards you.

In Richmond's 1972 preliminary final against St Kilda, there were a number of times where I

LOOK MUM, NO HANDS: Ron Barassi wrote about me bouncing the ball and then appealing for holding the man (above) when I was tackled. It was then that umpires began penalising me for dropping the ball.

should have received free kicks for being held while not in possession. Looking back, I feel I was denied those free kicks because of Barassi's comments and the pressure on umpires. Other players got rid of the ball late, and they appealed, but they didn't have a reputation like mine, so they were awarded free kicks.

NEW TRICKS: After the clamp-down on me throwing the ball out in front, my future was questioned. But I adapted. I learned to accelerate away from packs (above) and zigzag my way towards goal.

Many people said the rule change would be the end of me as a player; that without the opportunity to bounce the ball and get that free kick, the rule change would prove to be my kryptonite. But I played for another 11 seasons, winning best and fairests in the premiership years of 1973 and '74 and media awards in both years.

I admit that throwing the ball out in front of me had become instinctive. I had to adapt, and I must say I did so very quickly. Instead of bouncing the ball, I accelerated away from the tackler and zigzagged my way forward.

I've been on the Laws of the Game Committee since 1994. We make recommendations after being presented with a great deal of research. The AFL Commission must ratify any recommendation before the committee's proposals are adopted. I must stress: all we do is make suggestions.

The most common misconception of the Laws of the Game Committee is that we institute changes all the time. But if you have a look at the rules of the game as written more than a century ago, you'll come to understand the excellent work of those original authors. Our brief is to work within their framework.

This may sound a bit harsh, but I don't think many football supporters understand the laws of the game. They certainly don't appreciate how difficult it is to umpire, particularly with so many players around the ball at any one time.

Players and coaches are full-time professionals, who have plenty of time to devise and practise ways of overcoming rules.

That said, football owes a great deal to Mark Williams. He was the coach of Port Adelaide when he made an impressive presentation to the Laws of the Game Committee about the safety of players whose heads were over the ball. We should never forget the importance of his initial step.

One of the most significant changes made in the history of the game is the increased effort in the 2000s to protect the player bending over the ball. The rule now clearly states that a player cannot be taken out front on. If he is, then he gets a free kick and the player who made the contact most likely will be reported.

It was brought in because the AFL medical officers addressed the committee and expressed their concern for the safety of players. They said they were relieved and surprised that we had not had any injuries like the one that befell Footscray player Neil Sachse in 1975.

In just his second senior game, Sachse was left paralysed for life after an in-play, accidental clash with Fitzroy's Kevin O'Keeffe.

I believe that players and supporters appreciate that rule. If they don't, they should think again, because it was created for the health and welfare of the players. I'd like to think we all believe that, while football should remain a contact sport, the safety of the player must be recognised.

The evolution of the 'marking' law is a good example of how the committee observes the game and understands its evolution and makes recommendations to enhance the game or restore

STRETCHER, PLEASE: The AFL's Laws of the Game Committee has tried to ensure that concussed players receive the right treatment.

the intention of the original lawmakers. In the 1859 Rules of Football, it is written that *"Pushing with the hands or body is allowed ... except in the case provided in point 6."* And point 6 is ... when a player is marking.

What we do on many occasions is simply reinforce what was written long ago. As the game changes and tactics evolve, things are let go. Players take a small advantage, then push the limits and before long rules are being interpreted differently to those expressed in the laws of the game.

Take marking as an example. In the 1980s players started taking spectacular marks after elevating themselves in part by putting their hands on opponents' backs or shoulders. Umpires paid those marks because they were loath to penalise a player after such a big leap. Champion umpire Bill Deller once told me as much.

In recent years, we've reached a point where footy reflects a game of keepings-off. There might be 200 marks in a game but only 20 are contested. Players would rather handball backwards than kick to a contest.

We on the Laws committee were reluctant to look on as a great aspect of the game died. We want one-on-one contests where the player in front is afforded every opportunity and the player behind him can use his body or place his knee in the back and elevate himself up without putting his hands in the other player's back.

There's too much grey area if the defending player is allowed to use his hands; it leaves the umpire to make the difficult call as to whether the player behind gained extra leverage by using his hands.

No one put his hands in the back in the old days when taking great marks. Consider the career of Peter Hudson. He was a big man who simply turned side-on to bump off an opponent who was edging back towards him. Hudson would never ever have thought about putting his hands in the back. John Coleman, Alex Jesaulenko and Michael Roach all just ran and jumped.

HANDS OFF: Bygone champs like Alex Jesaulenko (top) managed to get a lift without using their hands. Matthew Richardson, however, wasn't happy when he took a mark in the 2008 Dreamtime game but was penalised for putting his hands in his opponent's back.

ON-OFF SWITCH: The move to limit rotations by introducing a substitute has been embraced by fans and denounced by coaches.

The hands-in-the-back rule increased one-on-one contested marks by only a small margin, but at least it helped to stop a great feature of the game from becoming extinct. But guess what? Coaches are now trying to outsmart the Laws committee again. They are nearly to the point now of instructing players to avoid kicking to contests. To them kicking to a contest is a last resort. And what an absolute shame that is for this great game.

I am really passionate in my belief that the high mark will never return as a permanent highlight in our game. It is dead. Players are so skilful, and the keepings-off nature of the game so ingrained, that players don't release the ball until they are all but sure they can find a target.

People go crook at the Laws committee for trying to speed up the game, when simply we are trying to reduce the number of stoppages and bring continuity into the game.

I recall one game in which there were 70 stoppages. Let's say that each stoppage chews up about 10 seconds each. That equates to 700 seconds, or about 13 minutes of the game. We felt that by encouraging continuous play, stoppages would decrease and the ball would stay in motion.

So the slight rule changes included:
- allowing players to kick in straight away following a behind;
- allowing only six seconds after a mark has been taken before play on is called;
- allowing a maximum of 30 seconds for a set shot
- forcing players who dive on the ball to knock the ball out.

However, the coaches will always seek ways to outsmart the Laws committee. That is a level that we never considered. That will always be so, and the Laws committee must be just as alert to retain the truth of the game.

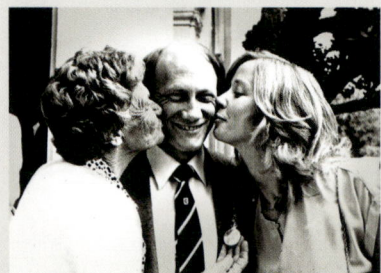

Order of Australia

I became a member of the Order of Australia for services to football after receiving a letter on June 4, 1981, just before my 350th game. I was invited to Government House and brought along my mother and my wife. Sir John Winneke presented the medal to me. Whenever I wear a jacket I always wear the AM badge. I am very proud of the award, and my country.

PERSONAL AND CONFIDENTIAL

Government House,
Canberra 2600.

4 JUN 1981

Dear Mr Bartlett,

Further to my earlier letter His Excellency the Governor-General has asked me to let you know that your nomination for appointment as a Member of the Order of Australia has been approved by Her Majesty The Queen.

Your award will be published in the Press on 13 June 1981, and in the Commonwealth of Australia Gazette on the same day. It would be appreciated if you would continue to treat this matter as strictly confidential un the day of publication. From that date you will be entit to use the initials A.M. after your name.

In due course you will be invited to attend an Investiture at which you will be presented with your Insignia.

The Governor-General has asked me to convey his congratulations, to which I would like to add my

Yours sincerely,

(David I. Smith)
Official Secretary to the Governor-General

Page 2 — The Sun, Saturday, June 13, 1981

Tiger Kev scores a new honor

RICHMOND rover Kevin Bartlett, 34, is a member of the Order of Australia in the Queen's Birthday Honors list.

He receives the award for service to football.

In a career that started 16 years ago, Bartlett has played in 350 games and scored 658 goals, including five last Saturday.

He has played in five premierships and represented Victoria 14 times.

A father of three, Bartlett said yesterday: "This is a wonderful surprise, a great thrill. It's one of the great moments of my life.

"It's got to be one of the highest points of my career, if not the highest.

"All we need now is to win the flag to ...

team, said the "terrific surprise" could not have come at a better time.

"I have been a bit low with the lack of cricket, hospital and pneumonia so this has provided a real spur for me," he said.

"I believe this is probably a team award.

"I am proud that people have thought of me and I will be happy to accept the award."

Lillee, 32 next month, and holder of the Australian Test wicket-taking record at 251 up to last season, hopes he ...

MBE for service to swimming.

The Victorian RSL president, Mr Bruce Ruxton, receives an OBE for services to Australian veterans and the RSL for 30 years.

Also honored in the list are two of Australia's top intelligence agents, Mr Bob Furlonger, who is made a companion of the Order of the Bath, and Mr Ian Kennison receives a CBE.

Mr Furlonger, former director-general of the National Assessments and Joint Intelligence Organisation retired recent-...

Mr Kennison, a former ...

WARMEST CONGRATULATIONS FOR THE HONOUR WHICH THE QUEEN HAS CONFERRED ON YOU
MALCOLM FRASER

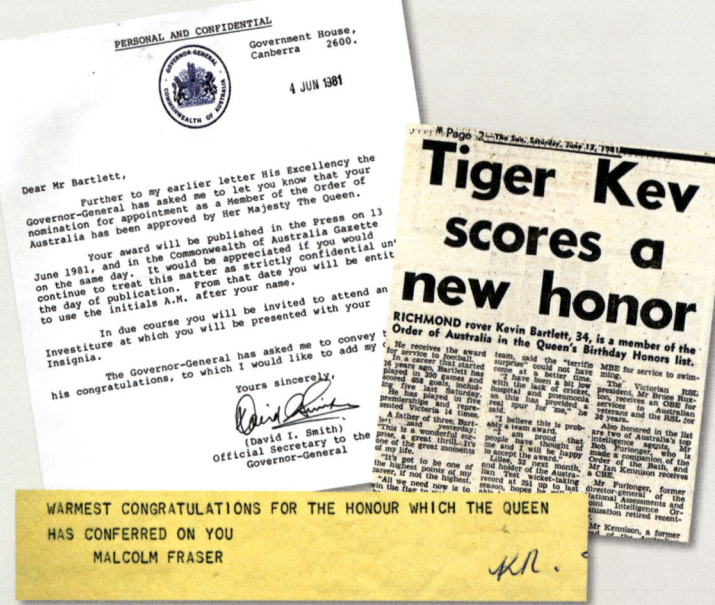

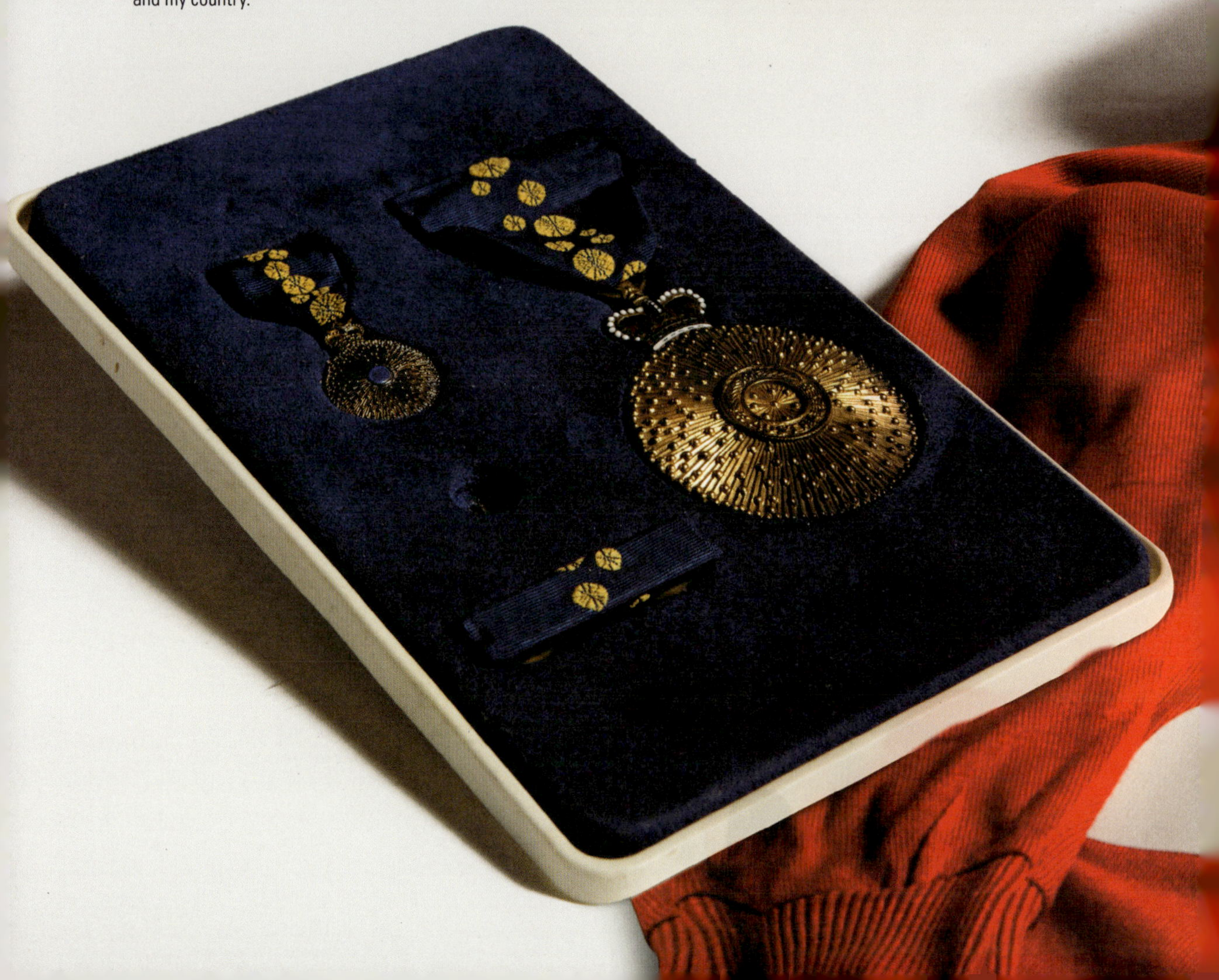

Big Birthday Party

On May 8, 1996, to celebrate the League's centenary, I took part in a re-enactment game on the MCG, in which a bunch of old-timers dressed as they would have 100 years ago. We were fatter and slower than in our prime, but it was tremendous fun.

This photo was taken before the re-enactment game in 1996. I'm in the front row and decided to pose as they did a century ago, stretching out without an apparent care in the world.
BACK: (from left) Gary Pert, Barry Breen, David Cloke, Peter McKenna, Bernie Quinlan, Russell Greene, Francis Bourke, Peter Knights, Michael Tuck, Peter Bedford, Kelvin Moore.
CENTRE: Peter Hudson, Peter Daicos, Robert DiPierdomenico, Leigh Matthews, Don Scott, Graham Arthur, Maurice Rioli, Dermott Brereton, John 'Sam' Newman.
FRONT: John Birt, Doug Hawkins, Garry Wilson, Jack Clarke, Kevin Bartlett, Kevin Murray, Gary Buckenara.

ON THE AIR: Hamming it up in the studio.

KB
WATCHING THE GAME

HUNGRY FOR THE MEDIA

I was mad keen on sport and I wanted to work in sport when my playing days were over. The media seemed a good idea, and so it's proved to be.

Like many high-profile footballers, I began my first regular media commitment while I was still playing. It was at the now-defunct *Sporting Globe* where my brief was to write a weekly article about forthcoming games and opponents. I would go into the offices in the city on a Sunday morning and dictate my article to *Globe* journalist Greg Hobbs.

In my final year as a player, 1983, I was a panellist on a radio show on 3UZ on a Friday afternoon. It was a preview of the weekend's games called *The Sunicrust Football Show*. My old under-19s coach, Ray Jordon, was also on the panel. Leon Wiegard, a long-time media personality and a former president of Fitzroy, hosted the show.

Around that time, 3UZ created a drive-time show called *Sports Talk*. Wiegard hosted on Monday and Friday, while the late Ian Cleland, a former umpire, did the show on Tuesday and Thursday. I was asked if I could appear on the Wednesday show.

At the time, Richmond trained every Monday, Tuesday and Thursday so I was available. The host was Craig Willis, who was later renowned as the master of ceremonies for the AFL the voice of the AFL and the Australian Open.

Bob Cornish was the 3UZ station manager. He approached me and asked if I would consider hosting the show five days a week. I was keen on the idea and accepted immediately, which meant leaving

MY FIRST COLUMN: For the *Sporting Globe*, on February 2, 1981.

Telecom (now Telstra), where I had been working as an instrument-maker since I was 15.

I was mad keen on sport and I wanted to maintain an involvement in sport after retiring as a player, so it wasn't a difficult decision to swap the instruments for a microphone.

My TV career came about because of a speech I gave at the Jack Dyer Roast in 1982. I gave a speech about Jack's style of commentating and told a few Richmond stories, such as my take on the infamous Windy Hill brawl in 1974.

Ron Casey, the host of Channel Seven's iconic Sunday afternoon show, *World of Sport*, approached me after the roast. He said he wanted me to join *World of Sport* after I retired.

The show's panel boasted esteemed characters like Jack Dyer, Lou Richards, Bob Davis, Neil Roberts, Peter McKenna, 'Crackers' Keenan and John 'Sammy' Newman. In 1984 I joined them as a regular. I interviewed the coaches on 'Coaches Corner' and I fetched the footballs during the handball competition.

It was wonderful experience to be part of such a famous show, but nobody gave me any feedback. No brickbats, no bouquets, not a thing. It was simply a matter of watching a game every Saturday, turning up on the set the next day and getting straight into it.

I soon came to understand – and it still holds true today – that you don't get too much advice when you're on TV. You are left to your own resources.

In 1984, 3UZ decided to get out of race-calling, which was a momentous decision because it had been the station's bread and butter through its existence. There had long been stories about crosses from the football late in a close game to broadcast the tote dividends from a country race meeting. Under the new regime, there would be music and an uninterrupted call of the footy, and it was my job to put together a broadcasting team.

So I recruited the great Mike Williamson, who had virtually been in retirement since the late 1970s, to be my co-commentator. I felt he had such vast knowledge and experience in broadcasting that he would really help me learn the ropes.

I also got a former Richmond teammate, Brian 'The Whale' Roberts, as our special comments man. Whale had a unique and colourful way of expressing himself. I recruited Stuart Magee, who had been captain of Footscray as well as a former South Melbourne player. Then there were two

LISTEN IN: Articles announcing my radio moves: *TV Scene*, February 1982.

 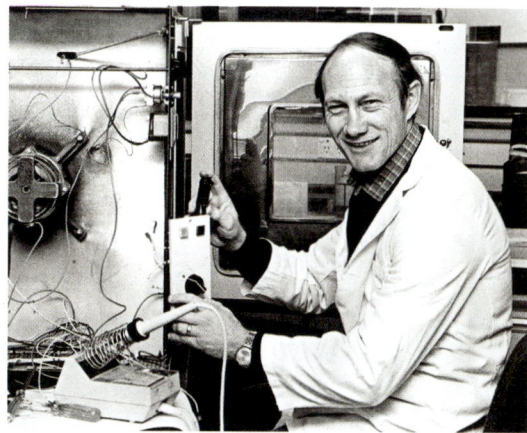

OLD HANDS: Ron Casey (left), Lou Richards and Jack Dyer always had something brewing on *World of Sport*. The photo on the right shows me working as an instrument-maker at Telecom. It was the job I had from the age of 15 until my media career took over in the mid-1980s.

former Carlton wingmen, Phil Pinnell and Brian Quirk. We also had Neville Fields, a very good player for Essendon and South Melbourne, while Bryan Wood, formerly of Richmond and Essendon, came to the team later on. Our statistician was George McHutchison, a lifelong friend who I knew from my playing days at Richmond.

In addition to the match broadcasts, we had a Sunday morning wrap show in which we talked about the highlights of the round, and I continued to do sports reports on the news throughout the week.

I was as busy in the media as I ever was while juggling my playing career with a full-time job at Telecom.

The broadcasting went for a couple of years before 3UZ was sold in 1986, which, as I learned early on, seems to happen often in radio. As a result, there was no more football; instead the station focused country and western music.

Luckily I was still doing *World of Sport*. I branched further into TV by co-hosting, with Sandy Roberts, a great Saturday morning show called *The Junior Supporters Club*.

My role was to catch up with footballers and do comedy sketches with them. My routines were ahead of their time. I remember meeting Mark Thompson while he was playing at Essendon and working as an electrician and we were able to pretend, with the help of a graphics department, that he and I pressed a few wrong buttons and accidentally blew up a few buildings. The skit ended with both of us covered in rubble.

My schtick was to chance across footballers as I went about my daily life. They'd be plumbers, butchers, real estate agents — somehow I'd just bump into them, do and interview and then something would always go wrong. It was very *Get Smart*.

In one episode I confused the Osborne brothers (Fitzroy's Richard and Graham) for the musical act the Osmond Brothers. So I was playing the guitar and they were landscaping and I somehow ended up chopping trees with my guitar. My car boot contained props to use for the episodes, such as guitars, caps, spanners, cricket bats and tennis racquets. My old Holden Commodore would always get a cameo in the show much like Peter Falk's car in Columbo.

I interviewed Fitzroy's Jamie Cooper before he became famous for doing football-related paintings. At the time, he was a young artist doing caricatures and working for a graphic designer.

I interviewed Hawthorn's Russell Morris at a large petrol station at which he worked. The sketch was that I pulled up my car and began interviewing him. I got distracted, and while I thought I was

PART OF THE TEAM: Raising a storm (top) on the *Junior Supporters Club* with North's Mark Arceri; above is the article welcoming me to *The Sun*'s team on March 15, 1985; my column dinkus.

refuelling my car I was refuelling a large petrol tanker beside me. The final bill came to $3000!

These shows were broadcast so long ago that I still have them on BETA tape.

Then I went to 3DB, where my show was promoted as 'Hear KB on DB'. It was a drive program five days a week. My panel operator was Andrew Bensley, who is now a well-known racing correspondent. The station was under the old *Herald* building in Flinders Lane. At the time 3DB was a racing station, so crosses from all around Australia often interrupted my show. Keith McGowan, later famous for working overnights at 3AW, was doing all the race results. In theory, I was doing a sports drive show in between race meetings.

The show didn't last long because again the station got sold. Bert Newton was brought in to be the general manager as well as the host of the morning program. Bert informed Danny Finley, my manager at the time, that I wouldn't be required because the station was going to become a talk station and at 4 o'clock they wanted to do a current affairs-style program instead.

Danny rang me when I was on the set of *World of Sport*. Bert interviewed me once on his show *Good Morning Australia*. I brought up my sacking from 3DB and it inspired a great deal of mirth.

I've been on many talk and variety shows: the Don Lane Show, the Roy and HG Show, *This Is Your Life with Kevin Sheedy* — I've even appeared on a celebrity episode of *Family Feud*. My team included Robert DiPierdomenico and Tom Hafey. To this day, I have no idea how the game worked. There was no practice run. We just flew up to Sydney and did the show. Our team lost. As a consolation prize, I received a diary.

In 1987, the journalist and producer Stephen Phillips approached me. Stephen at that stage was working at 3AK. He wanted to set up a football team for 3AK (then part of Kerry Packer's media interests) to cover the VFL in its first season as a national competition; it was the season when West Coast and the Brisbane Bears started up. I thought it would be great, so I accepted the offer.

I started by doing some sports updates on the morning show with John Blackman. Then I set about setting up the commentary team. Phillips and I were going to call the matches while Don Scott, Doug Wade, 'Crackers' Keenan and Bryan Wood would do the special comments.

We unveiled the team at a launch at the 3AK offices in the Channel 9 complex in Bendigo Street, Richmond. We did practice calls at Waverley Park during a pre-season match. We even put our groundsmen in different parts of the ground and pretended to cross 'live' to them at another venue.

During the week leading up to the opening round, Kerry Packer accepted an outrageous offer from Alan Bond to buy Channel 9 and 3AK. Soon afterwards it was announced that 3AK's proposed football broadcasts were to be axed; 3AK was going to revert to being a music station because it was more cost-effective. I had to ring up the other members of team and tell them that our football show would never get to air.

OVER THE JOURNEY: Tom Hafey (left), Rhett, Kevin Sheedy and me on the set of *This Is Your Life*. Sheeds was the show's subject.

TIGER ON THE TELLY: Robert DiPierdomenico interviews me on *AFL Squadron* during my coaching career.

At the start of that year, Channel 7 had lost the rights to the football to a company called Broadcom, and the ABC had acquired some of the games for live broadcasts.

I listened to the season's opening game, North Melbourne v Brisbane Bears, on the radio. On the Sunday, I watched the game the ABC was broadcasting. The commentators were Tim Lane and Doug Heywood, with special comments from Gary Dempsey. Their show was called ... *The Footy Show*!

I had known Gary for many years. I knew he had a husky and thin voice because of vocal cord damage caused during his great career at Footscray and North Melbourne.

He had been hit across the throat in play. It seems no one had asked Gary about this. When they threw to him during the broadcast, it was very hard to hear what he was saying.

On the Monday morning Tim Lane called to advise me that Gary would be unable to continue to do special comments. He was wondering whether I would like to do it. What an opportunity! I had a great year travelling around the country with Tim Lane and the great Doug Heywood. I was writing for *The Sun* at the time, too.

The ABC had a weekly football program hosted by Drew Morphett, with Ron Barassi, Leigh Matthews and me previewing matches. I also called a couple of games for the ABC. I remember one day calling the Carlton v Geelong game, with Clarke Hansen and John Nicholls making special comments.

At the end of 1987, a few clubs approached me about coaching. There were strong expressions of interest from Melbourne and Fitzroy and mild interest from Footscray. While I was very tempted, my love had always been for the Richmond Football Club. If ever there was an opportunity to coach the Tigers, I planned to take it. That opportunity arose after the 1987 season. I took the coaching role and relinquished all my media commitments.

When I finished coaching Richmond at the end of 1991 I had no job for six months, which was tough on the family because I had three kids going through private schools.

I was fortunate that 3AW asked me to join their team as a part-time caller and around-the-grounds man with Sam Newman. I also started doing sports reports on the breakfast program with Ross Stevenson and Dean Banks.

That was very enjoyable as Ross and Dean were both outstanding men to work with. I gave away Krosno glasses each morning as a prize for a quiz question. I also did a 'Kev's Rev of the Day', where I would give a pep talk based, somehow, around a carton of Rev milk. And occasionally, when Ross and Dean were away, I co-hosted the show with Greg Evans.

At this stage, Sam Newman had been through some hard times. He had gone broke and was working his way back up. But that didn't stop him being tremendous fun, particularly when our around-the-ground equipment didn't work. Sam Newman had no patience and little generosity. I had to carry around this big silver box that contained all the broadcast equipment because Sam refused to carry it.

When we got to the ground we had to plug in the box and test the level, talking to the panel operator back in the studio. Often, for whatever reason, it wouldn't work. And then Sam would do this hilarious routine of how we can put a man on the moon yet we can't speak to someone from the Western Oval.

There were many times when Sam said, 'If we are not connected within 12 minutes, I am leaving.' If we were having technical difficulties during a game, he would just sit there and refuse to talk.

There were times when our around-the-ground box at Kardinia Park was situated out in the crowd. That upset Sam immensely. The box could get freezing cold and it was barely under cover. But more than that, it was right underneath the siren. Sam seemed to always be talking just as the siren blared.

After the game, it was the custom for around-the-grounds people to go down to the rooms to get some interviews, then come back to the box and hang around for talkback. More often than not, no one rang up with a question about the around-the-grounds game.

So here was Sam, me and my son Rhett, the only ones left at Kardinia Park, freezing to death, hoping a listener would ring in. Often we'd just had enough. Twenty minutes before the end of the post-match show, we would ask the panel operator to tell the main game's callers, Rex Hunt and Shane Healy that we were heading off. On the way back, we always stopped off at the McDonald's just past the footy ground.

I remember Sam and I were at the last game at Moorabbin in 1992 between St Kilda and Fitzroy.

TOP OF THE HEAP: In 1993, I was on 3AW's broadcasting team with (from left) Ron Barassi, Rex Hunt, Sam Newman and Shane Healy.

TOP SCORE: A copy of the *Football Record* (top) showing Jason Dunstall's 17 goals against Richmond in round 7, 1992. Note the method of marking the goals: the number correlates to the quarter in which the score was recorded. For example, 3 denotes a goal or behind in the third quarter. Dunstall also kicked five behinds in that match. The League record of 18 goals was set by Melbourne's Fred Fanning in 1947.

Rhett ran on the ground after the match, dug up a piece of ground, put it in a paper cup and brought it back to the commentary box where Sam proceeded to describe it in fine detail over the air.

We were also broadcasting the day Jason Dunstall kicked 17 goals against the Tigers at Waverley Park. We kept referring to the threat to Fred Fanning's record of 18 goals while Sam talked about Dunstall being too unselfish, handballing and paddling the ball on instead of kicking as many goals as possible.

On some occasions Dunstall ran down the ground following his man out of the forward line and Sam would yell out from the commentary box for him to go back and get the record!

Rex Hunt was calling at another match and he just said down the line that Sam and I should speak over him if at any stage Dunstall looked like kicking his 18th goal. Well near the end of the game it almost happened, so I said on air, 'Come to us, come to us."

They crossed to us, I was commentating, the ball on the way up forward but Dunstall had two men on him. All you could then hear was Sam yelling, "It doesn't matter, just pass it to him."

Famously, Sam and I broadcast a finals match between West Coast and Hawthorn in Perth. 3AW sent no one else to the game, just Sam and me. I went across by myself because Sam was coming from Queensland where he had been on a holiday playing golf. So we met up at the airport in Perth and there was Sam in his shorts and carrying his golf bag.

We got a taxi straight to the game, where I was to do all the broadcasting and Sam was to do all the special comments. For me, it was one of the great days of broadcasting. We had the time of our lives. We were grabbing guests from neighbouring media boxes, just trying to do a pre-game show on the run, on our own, because we had no producer.

Our broadcast box was pretty archaic. There was a great piece of concrete across the roof of the broadcast area. The game had only just started when Sam got very excited and jumped up and just about knocked himself out on the concrete. He was dazed for the entire game. He had no idea what he was

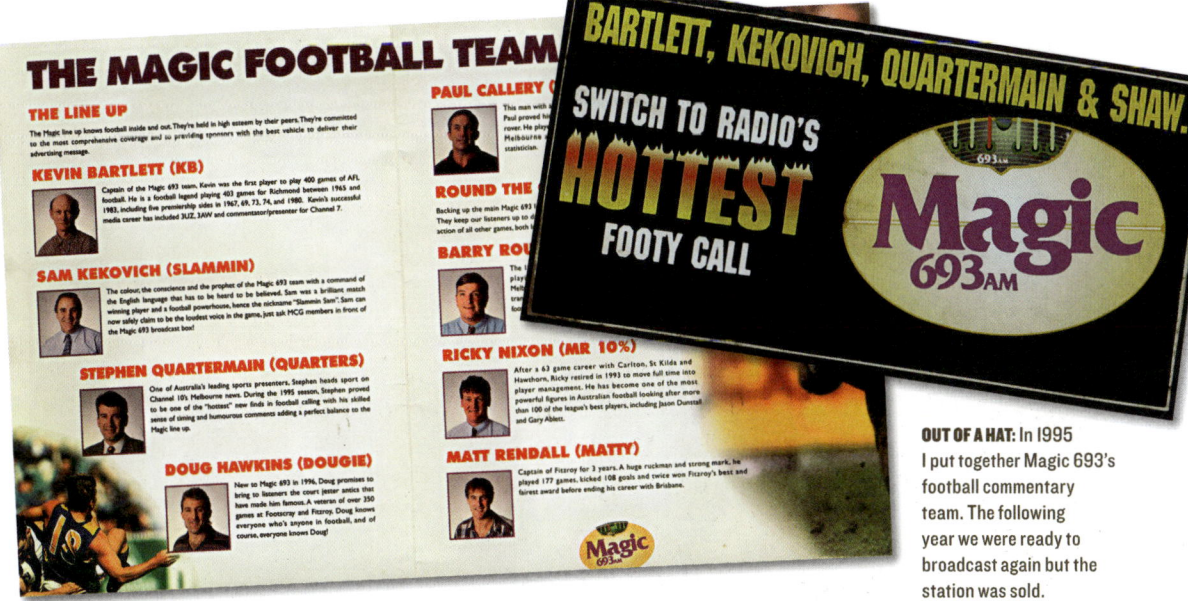

OUT OF A HAT: In 1995 I put together Magic 693's football commentary team. The following year we were ready to broadcast again but the station was sold.

saying. I remember I announced on air that, 'Sam Newman has knocked himself out.'

After the game, Sam decided that we shouldn't hang around Perth; we should go home as soon as possible. So we went out to the airport and sat there until finally we convinced someone to give us to seats on an early flight. We were on the absolute last seats on the back of the plane, flying to Melbourne after midnight.

These days working with Sam was the most most fun for my son Rhett, who always tagged along, and for me too. To this day, we always talk about working with Sam. In 1992 the AFL dubbed a Collingwood versus Carlton game as 'The Match of the Century'. The match was to be held 100 years to the day since the two clubs first met. It was at the MCG under lights. 3AW had every possible broadcaster in the box, so much so that I was credited as 'extra special comments'. I barely was able to get a dozen sentences in.

During my time at 3AW, I commentated with Rex Hunt, Shane Healy and a game or two with Anthony Hudson. In fact I remember Anthony's first game as a broadcaster was opposite Gary Brice and me. There was a preliminary final on in Perth between Melbourne and the West Coast Eagles in 1994. We commentated on that game because the main commentary team was doing Geelong versus North Melbourne at the MCG.

On one occasion we lost the broadcast signal during a Friday night game at the MCG, so Shane Healy, Graeme Bond and I called a quarter of football through a mobile phone, just passing it around the box.

Another time, I was broadcasting the 1993 State of Origin match between Tasmania and Queensland at Hobart's Bellerive Oval. My co-commentators were Shane Healy and Gary Brice. There was no commentary box, so they ran a lead from a phone into the crowd and we stood there and called the game. Peter Cameron was the umpire that day. I had played many games with Peter as umpire, and of course Peter's brother-in-law was David Cloke.

So at half-time, as the umpires were walking off the ground through the tunnel, which was just beside us, I yelled out, on air, 'You're killing Tasmania, you've never been ever good, you killed Richmond and you never gave David Cloke a free kick.' He looked up and replied, 'Get stuffed, Bartlett.' The crowd around us thought the entire broadcast was hilarious.

TELEVISION DAYS: I thoroughly enjoyed working at Channel 7 with Bob Davis (centre) and Sandy Roberts.

Rex's style was very colourful and entertaining, even if it was a boring match.

Shane Healy was his ideal sidekick because he was a straight, matter-of-fact caller. Ron Barassi did special comments. When Ron got the job of coaching Sydney, Sam was elevated to the main commentary team. This gave Sam the chance to show his ability to be clever, funny and confrontational. That commentary team was a fantastic combination.

In 1994, Magic 693, a station that was playing old songs, asked if I would start up a new football team. They had done football broadcasts the year before with the late Ian Major and Dwayne Russell but that team had ended. I thought it would be a great thrill to set up a football team again, so I accepted.

Around this time, I told Ross Stevenson and Dean Banks from the breakfast show of my intention to leave the station. Ross saw this as some sort of sign, so in the Melbourne Cup that year, 1994, he put a box trifecta on 6, 9, 3 – Magic's call sign. And the final standings of the Cup were: Jeune (3), Paris Lane (6) and Oompala (9). I couldn't believe it. I didn't have money on it, but every time I think of the call sign I think of the 1994 Melbourne Cup.

The year at Magic 693 was one of the most enjoyable in my radio career. I had been a fan of Stephen Quartermain on television. Ricky Nixon had a role with the previous Magic broadcast team and he suggested that Stephen would be a great caller next to me. And I never doubted Ricky, so we hired Stephen and he was just fantastic.

I also went out to Collingwood training one day and spoke to the then assistant coach Tony Shaw. He was a former Magpies premiership captain and Norm Smith Medal winner and I knew he would bring a lot to the broadcast in terms of his knowledge in the game. So he agreed to do special comments on the days when Collingwood wasn't playing. He was tremendous. Tony Shaw is very much a people's person. He was fantastic with the audience when we had outside broadcasts. He loved to get contestants up from the crowd and he kept everyone entertained.

Finally, I was looking for someone who was colourful, knew a lot about the game, could fill in for special comments when Tony wasn't there, and perhaps could call a few games, because I was still calling football on Channel 7. We looked at a number of people at that stage: Warwick Capper, Mark Jackson and – at Ricky Nixon's suggestion – Sam Kekovich.

Mark was a very good player, he had some original thoughts on football and he was very colourful. He showed great potential but he did have a lot of commitments on his plate, plus he was a bit more expensive than the budget allowed.

We also spoke to Warwick. My memory is that Warwick was very excited about doing it, but he wanted to know if he could pre-record his special comments. Then we could just push a button during a broadcast and play his comments. Who knows whether Warwick was fair dinkum? We said no.

So I spoke to Sam Kekovich and it was one of the best decisions I ever made. At this stage Sam wasn't doing a great deal in football; he was just working for a computer company. Like Tony Shaw, Sam straight away brought enthusiasm and the fun he brought to the team. Think of his TV advertisements and his guest speaking – that was Sam and his commentary. We were able to experience all of that in the first year of Magic 693's broadcast.

We created a segment called 'On the Couch with Keka' as part of our lead-in. The idea was that he would ask a series of silly questions to current and former players.

The questions were always written by Rhett Bartlett and included gems like, 'What animal was the Canary Islands named after?' (The answer is Dogs.) Or: 'Who was the millionaire on Gilligan's Island?' (Thurston Howell III.) And we started to experience the magnificent language and phrasing that Keka brought to football. Tony Shaw called a game with us alongside Ricky Nixon in Sydney one day. Ricky also called a game over in Adelaide alongside Keka and he reckons the first time listeners heard him was halfway through the third quarter – Keka just did not come up for breath.

We had Matt Rendell and Barry Round as around-the-ground commentators and our statistician was Paul Callery, my runner from my days as Richmond coach. Paul was a lecturer in sports science and a great person to have around. We gave him the nickname 'The Count'. On our first broadcast, he introduced a new stat in football – the one per centers. It was not done in those days to record stats for blocks, shepherds and knock-ons. Now every radio broadcaster refers to them.

Keka was great with the crowd at the MCG. He would hang his head out of the broadcast box and yell at the spectators and they would yell back. One day he threw money into the crowd.

He was such a huge figure that, on many occasions, the 3AW broadcast box would knock on our door and complain that Keka's voice was leaking through into the effects mike of 3AW. This was a bit cheeky considering they had Rex in their box! Keka just called the game more loudly.

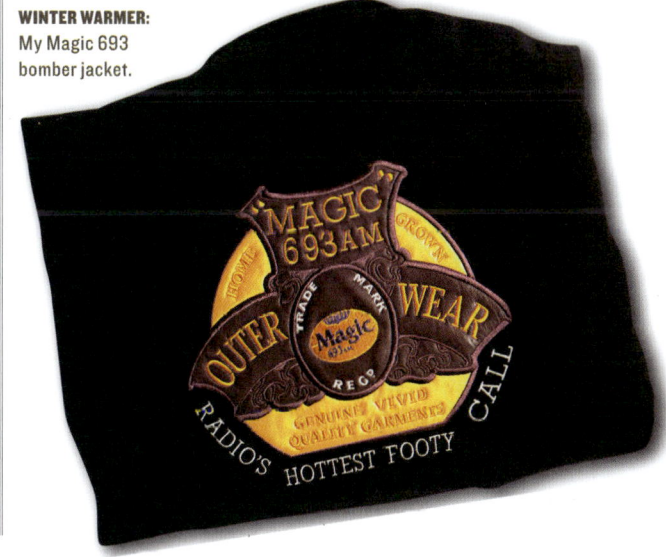

WINTER WARMER: My Magic 693 bomber jacket.

The first time the Magic team did a practice run was a night Grand Final at Waverley Park. The AFL would not let us broadcast, so we did a phantom call, with everyone there apart from one person: Keka. I have no idea where he was. We put Rhett in his seat to pretend we were throwing to Keka. Many spectators that night said they couldn't pick us up on the radio, so we knew the interest was there from the audience.

The most amazing broadcast day on Magic 693 was the 1995 State-Of-Origin match in which Ted Whitten did his final lap of honour. I will never forget that day. We all knew Ted was very ill and there was talk he wasn't going to be there on that day. Many didn't realise the extent of his illness. When he came out in the car and began his circuit of the ground with his son Ted Junior, I began broadcasting with Stephen Quartermain and Sam Kekovich.

I was trying to paint the picture of Ted jnr in the car with him, the roar of the crowd, the fact that this may be the last time Ted could attend a match, and the touching moment when he rested his head on young Ted's shoulder. As I was describing the lap I found myself becoming emotional, so I threw to Quarters: 'This is a moment no one at this ground will ever forget, something we may never see again, Quarters'. And there was silence. I looked over to Quarters and he had tears streaming down his face. I turned to Keka and he had tears streaming down his face. It was the most emotional moment I have experienced in a broadcast box.

At the end of the game, all the media folk were talking in the media room when the news began on the TV in the corner. The bulletin led with the E.J. Whitten lap. I kid you not, every single radio broadcaster was looking up at this small TV in the corner of the roof and not a single word was spoken for five minutes.

Magic 693 was the first football broadcaster to have a song written specifically for us to promote the members of our team. It was written and performed by Colleen Hewitt. I approached Colleen through Danny Finley. She wrote this fantastic song.

> Hear the roar, it's Tony Shaw.
> Stephen Quartermain and The Count.
> Slammin' Sam, now come on KB, we're hungry
>   for our footy news, it's Magic.
> Sit right down and stay, with KB's footy team,
>   on Magic.
> They'll tell you all the news, impress you with
>   their views.
> You'll never miss a kick with KB, on Magic.

Rival broadcasters introduced music to their broadcasts the following year.

We rated as high as nine during Magic's first year of football, and the station wanted me to host a 6-7pm weeknight sports show. I had just started doing so when word came through that the station had been sold to Southern Cross, which also owned 3AW.

Southern Cross approached me to continue the football on Magic under the Southern Cross banner but the station was not going to do every match. I felt that, because 3AW was very important to Southern Cross, there would be little emphasis on the Magic football team. I felt we wouldn't be given the same opportunities as 3AW.

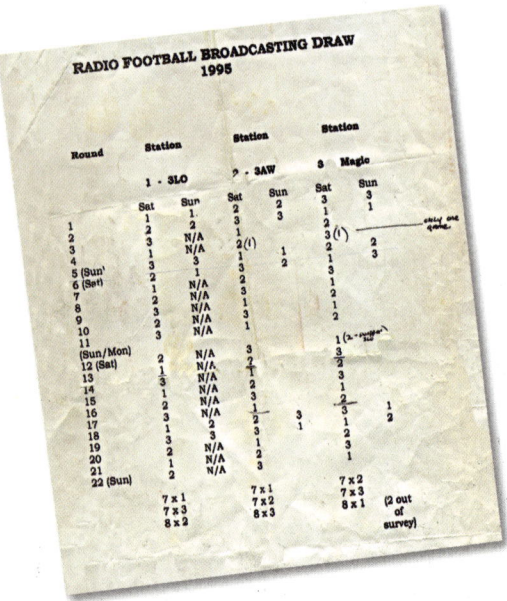

POLITICS: Southern Cross took over Magic late in 1995. I quit Magic because I suspected it would play second fiddle to 3AW every week.

MAGIC MOMENT: The most emotional moment of my broadcasting career: Ted Whitten's lap of honour before the State of Origin match between Victoria and South Australia at the MCG on June 17, 1995. Ted, pictured with his son Ted jnr during the lap of honour, died two months later.

For example, in those days we had to take picks each week to see which station would broadcast which game. I just suspected that, if Magic had a No.1 pick on a week with a blockbuster game, 3AW would take that choice and leave a lesser game to Magic.

All they said before the first edition of my evening show on Magic was, 'Just turn up tomorrow night and away we go.' I was worried that there would not be many to help me and just by chance I said to my Rhett, who was finishing Year 11, 'You better come with me, just in case we need a helping hand.' On the first show, there was the panel operator John Payne and me – no one to make calls or take calls. So it was fortunate that Rhett came along, because he ended up manning the phones and switching the guests through to the studio.

In the end I left Magic 693, taking with me great memories of a year of football broadcasting.

It's worth noting that during all this time on 3AW and Magic 693, I never went into the Richmond rooms to get an interview after the games. In fact, I have only been back to the Richmond dressing rooms once since my sacking as coach in 1991: to present a guernsey to Ben Griffiths before he made his debut against Port Adelaide in Adelaide in round 10, 2010.

I didn't realise it then but the decision to bail out of the Magic show turned out to be good one. 3UZ was about to change its name to Sport 927 and it was looking for a new breakfast program. Although they were a national racing station, they wanted a mornings breakfast sports program from 5.30-9am. They approached me through Danny Finley and they also approached Dr Turf (John Rothfield), who had worked with me briefly during 1994 at 3AW, when I was hosting a Saturday sports show from Midday to 6pm. We both signed with Sport 927.

Rick Wall had been the producer of the breakfast program but he decided to move into the newsroom, so they asked me whether I could suggest a producer. I recalled a young reporter I had worked with on the Magic 693 days. One weekday I needed to cross to someone at the tribunal to get an idea of what was happening.

I hunted around and found out that there was a reporter covering the tribunal for the *Herald Sun* by the name of Craig Hutchison. So I got him on to talk about what was happening and he did such a terrific job that I asked him to come on during the football broadcast each week and give us a sense of what was happening around the traps. He was entertaining, had his facts right and he exuded confidence.

Craig was to work as the producer of the breakfast show for nearly 10 months. Turfy, Craig and I had a terrific relationship; we got on marvelously well. Before the year was out, Craig was snapped up by Channel 10. Then of course he went to Channel 7 and then Channel 9.

Craig was a young guy who enjoyed the nightlife. I used to pick him up on the way to work. I'd get up at 4am and I'd pick him up around 4.20am – sometimes he was a little bit tardy. Sometimes when he was out late, he would go back to the radio station and sleep on the floor.

One morning, I got in at about 4.40am and I was sitting down reading the newspapers at a long desk and all of a sudden, like a jack in the box, his head popped up from under the desk. He scared the hell out of me.

For all that, he was a gun producer. He could track people down and he wasn't afraid to call people at 6.30am if they were on the back page of the paper. He got abused many times but he just soldiered on. He once told Rhett to keep trying Martina Navratilova's room overseas. He said to keep calling every 10 minutes.

Finally she answered at 1am and demanded to speak to the person who ordered the late calls. Craig got on the phone and managed to smooth things over and we did an interview the next day. He was persistent and would not stop for anything.

He contacted Neil Balme early on the morning after he was sacked as Melbourne coach. And, famously, he pre-recorded an interview with Bill Murray that is one of the funniest interviews ever. Doc and I were unavailable to do the interview, so Craig spoke to Murray about his films and the celebrity golf tournaments he played in.

Murray thought Craig was so terrible that he ended up asking if he really was a radio producer/presenter. He ended the interview abruptly by

BREAKFAST SERIAL: Promotional material for my Sport 927 show with co-hosts Dr Turf (top), Simon O'Donnell and Gary Honey.

RUCK KING: Striking a pose with Tiger great Roy Wright after Rhett had interviewed Roy for the 2008 centenary book.

telling Craig, 'You've got to work on your diction.' I did the breakfast show for eight and a half years. Turfy and I got on so well we have become close friends. We understood what each other was thinking so we always sounded very smooth. But Doc wasn't frightened to be controversial about the racing game, particularly when it came to betting, even though Tabcorp was a major sponsor of the station.

The program got several warnings that Dr Turf was getting very close to the bone but he refused to be silenced — until he went too far one morning talking about the bosses of Tabcorp. It was on a Friday. That afternoon I got a call from the station to say that Dr Turf had been sacked. That was very disappointing.

John Letts joined me for a short time and then Simon O'Donnell. Simon was great to work with, but he was very laid-back. He would get in just moments before the show and then start reading the paper when the show started. He was living at Kilmore. He lasted 12 months before the wear and tear became too great.

Then Gary Honey joined. An Olympic silver medallist in the long jump, he was a sports lover and he was fantastic for the show. He had an opinion on many sports and I really enjoyed teaming up with him. At the end of the year, I was told that Gary wouldn't be continuing as co-host. It was a great surprise to us both. To this day, neither of us really know the reason for his departure.

During this time I was also commentating with Channel 7. One game stands out.

It was Western Bulldogs versus Hawthorn in Auckland on January 29, 2000. Sandy Roberts and I were to travel to New Zealand to broadcast the game but for some reason we weren't able to get there. Instead it was decided we would call the game off the television screen at Channel 7. Sandy had been at the Australian Open at Melbourne Park all afternoon.

The match started and Sandy and I just went, 'Welcome to New Zealand, it's going to be a great game' and we spoke about the crowd and the weather as though we were under a long white cloud. This game was to be broadcast live, but there was a doubles match still going on at the Australian Open between Rick Leach and Ellis Ferreira and their opponents Wayne Black and Andrew Kratzmann.

So someone came down to tell us and said that we were to continue broadcasting. When the tennis was over they would simply cut into our match and broadcast from that point.

So we called the first quarter. At the end of the quarter, Channel 7 sports boss Gordon Bennett came down and said, 'You're not going to believe this, but the tennis has now gone to a fifth set, so just keep calling and we'll keep taping.'

We got to half-time and the tennis was still on. We got to three-quarter time and Gordon Bennett came down again and said the last set was still going. He said we would cross to the football to join the last quarter as soon as the tennis finished.

So midway through the last quarter, we got word through our headphones that the fifth set at the tennis had finished at 18-16 after 121 minutes. The bosses said they weren't going to cross to the football, but could we please keep calling.

So Sandy Roberts and I called an entire game of football from a television set in Channel 7 and only 10 minutes of highlights were shown. The match has never been seen in its entirety.

While I was doing the Sport 927 breakfast program, FOX Footy started up. Rick McKenna rang me to join as a football caller and be involved in a program called *Grumpy Old Men*, with Bob Davis, Doug Hawkins and Tony Shaw.

Five years of FOX Footy was great fun. I called the very first game broadcast on FOX Footy, alongside Jason Bennett. It was the Essendon v Sydney practice match at North Sydney in 2002 in which Tony Lockett returned to the AFL.

Grumpy Old Men was fantastic. Nothing was ever rehearsed. Stephen Phillips was the original producer, who was then replaced by Matthew Campbell. We always knew who was coming on, but we never discussed what questions we would ask and we never had a meeting to plan a segment. What you saw was as it was.

I would introduce who was on the program then I would throw to Bob, who would talk in his inimitable style about something that had made him grumpy over the weekend. Then the guest would come on and we would all ask questions.

The late Roy Simmonds from Hawthorn told great stories about playing under John Kennedy, but he also brought his banjo along and played a few songs. Both famous and forgotten players appeared, like Jack Collins, Peter Pianto, Ron Barassi, Alex Jesaulenko, John Goold, Bernie Quinlan, Michael Roach, Tom Hafey, Kevin Sheedy, Sam Kekovich, Geoff Raines, 'Diamond Jim' Tilbrook, Bruce McMaster-Smith, Carl Ditterich and Russell Renfrey. Viewers had not seen some of these former players on telly for more than 20 years!

We even did a special tribute on the day of the funeral of Jack Dyer. On our final show of the year, we had Leigh Matthews, singer Mike Brady talking about his footy songs, and Bill Green (aka WEG). People still stop me in the street and ask when *Grumpy Old Men* is coming back.

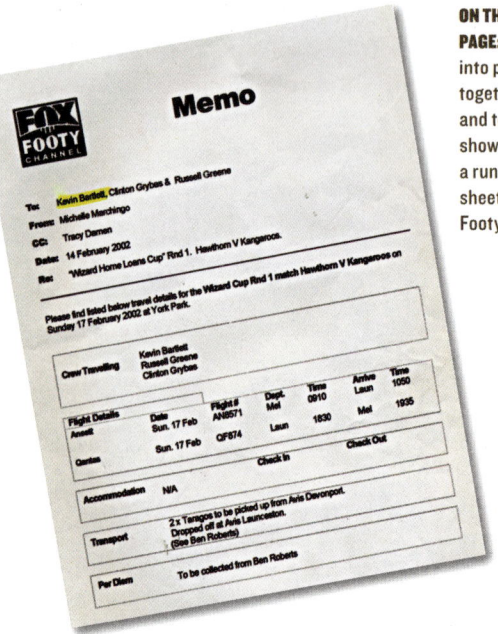

ON THE SAME PAGE: A lot goes into putting together radio and television shows. Here's a running sheet for a Fox Footy show.

IN MEMORY: I had the honour of delivering a eulogy for Jack Dyer, Richmond's most iconic figure, at his funeral at St Ignatius' Catholic Church in Richmond. Jack died on August 27, 2003, aged 89.

START UP: I left Sport 927 in 2004 to become SEN's first mornings broadcaster. It's exciting to be involved at a station devoted to sport.

As for my radio career, I left Sport 927 in 2004 to join SEN, a 24-hour sports station that was starting up. It was a very exciting to be involved in a station that was to be dedicated to sport. I was asked to do the morning program between 9am and midday. The person putting the station's programs together was Rod Law, a former 3AW producer who after setting up SEN's team, then joined Fox Sports as the director of its Melbourne office.

Our first day of broadcast was very sad because David Hookes had been badly hurt in a scuffle the previous night and was not expected to live. The first guest I had on my program was Ken Jacobs, who was running Victorian cricket at the time.

I've been doing a show on SEN for seven years now and I love it. The first couple of years the station didn't have rights to the football, which made it pretty tough. It nearly went bankrupt, the receivers were brought in, many presenters were not paid and others worked for nothing on occasions, but it was resurrected and it has gone from strength to strength. Most people seemed to think it would fail in the first few months. They were nearly right, but it survived. It has never been a place of egos. Everyone who has worked there has got on well with everyone else. It's been like a sporting family. It has always had a wonderful working atmosphere.

It is worth commenting on a handful of the broadcasters I've had the pleasure of calling football with on TV.

Sandy Roberts is a fantastic commentator. He hosted *World of Sport* and I worked with him on *Junior Supporters Club*. He was always so easy to work with, with a smile on his face. He is a generous broadcaster, who has no ego. I even did a short-lived revamped version of *League Teams* with him and Bob Davis.

I don't think Channel 7 put too much effort into it; it was just another show for them to list as they attempted to renegotiate the football rights. It was always disjointed, it didn't have any flow or balance to it.

We would tape the show late at night. I remember one particular night we had technical problems. We successfully recorded the first 15 minutes, but we encountered sound issues after that. It was so much of a schemozzle that we were still recording the last segment as the show was going to air.

I called with Clinton Grybas on FOX Footy and also appeared on his *White Line Fever* once a week. People talk about his commentating skills, but to me he truly shone when he was hosting. He was a tremendous young talent, who was knowledgeable, likeable, and well respected by the football media and by the players. There was nothing pretentious about him.

He just loved talking about sport and it was a great shock when he was found dead in his apartment. To this day, there seems to be no explanation.

It was terrific to commentate with Sandy Roberts, Bruce McAvaney and Dennis Cometti; I found them all fantastic to work with. They have lasted so long in the game because they're enjoyable to work with – always helpful, never wanting to hog the microphone.

The first game I broadcast on Channel 7 was a game between Adelaide and Footscray in Adelaide with Bruce. Bruce was so meticulous. He carried a huge hardcover book and wrote sporting results in it while we were on the plane – from soccer, to cycling to overseas athletic results. He kept his own records and annotated every page.

Bruce was always very generous. He always brought you into the conversation and the same applied to Dennis. Dennis was very laid-back, always with a good quirky one-liner. And he was very generous.

Case in point. When calling football, you call for an unspecified period of time and then you pass over to your broadcast colleague. You just know when it is best to throw; it becomes second nature. Sometimes you find yourself commentating for a slightly longer or shorter period than your co-commentator, depending on the passage of play.

One day I was calling with Dennis and he had to go to the toilet. While he was gone, North

LUNCH BUNCH: SEN's lunchtime footy panels in the suburbs (above) have been a great success. At left is the *AFL Record* from Fitzroy's final game. I got all the signatures from the Roys players on the flight home.

Melbourne kicked five goals in succession. When he came back, I made a few comments to help him pick up the play he had missed, like, 'Wow, what an amazing five minutes of football that was, Dennis, just goal after goal,' and I gestured for him to take the call. He just waved me away and motioned for me to keep calling. And I thought, 'No one has heard him for the last six or seven minutes. That is an example of how generous he is as a broadcaster.'

I called the last game at Waverley, between Sydney and Hawthorn, sitting next to Peter Landy. I was also broadcasting next to Peter Landy when he called his 1000th game! It was also out at Waverley.

I commentated on the last game of Fitzroy in 1996 with Drew Morphett. It was a sad day, but Fremantle gave the Roys a great send-off.

Late in 2010 my contribution to the media was recognised with induction as a Life Member of the AFL Media Association. I was thrilled. I've loved my three decades in the media. I hope to continue to play a role for years to come.

AFTERWORD
BY KEVIN BARTLETT

A LIFE IN FOOTBALL

The game has changed but it remains the biggest thing in my life and the lives of many others. I'm humbled by the sense of excitement and fulfilment it's given me. Long may it last.

When I look back on my football career, I realise my good fortune in arriving at the Richmond Football Club at a time when it was about to embark on its greatest era. It's amazing to think that in the space of one or two years players like Francis Bourke, Royce Hart, Michael Green, Dick Clay and Barry Richardson arrived at the club. It's also incredible that we were able to play together as a group for so long.

There have been so many great football players who just haven't been in the right place at the right time. Some play for so many seasons – maybe they win club honours – but they never reach the pinnacle of football.

It's fantastic to think that you played sport at the highest level with a group of friends. It's humbling to be reminded that you achieved your best in your chosen sport, and it's a constant pleasure our annual premiership players' get-together in Grand Final week to celebrate and reminisce about the days when we ruled the world.

I believe the Richmond Football Club of my era was such a powerful club because every player at Tigerland was so close. There were no egos, no one player was more important or considered better than the next; we were all treated equally.

It's remarkable to consider how much the game, and all that surrounds it, has changed from my day when we all had full-time jobs. Players were instrument-makers, plumbers, builders, bank tellers, carpenters and lawyers. Yet we'd turn up two or three days a week and train in poor conditions, on a muddy old ground that had little or no lighting, in ramshackle rooms.

But there was such tremendous camaraderie. No one played for the money or the benefits. You played for the love of the game.

GLORY DAYS: More mementoes including (from left) a duffel coat, a KB beer can (even though I'm a teetotaller), a photo with Kevin Bartlett the racing car driver, me as the King of Moomba in 1984, a cartoon in *The Sun* on June 6, 1981, and my club life-membership certificate.

A FAMILY AFFAIR: Standing (left to right): Cara (daughter), me, Luke (Cara's husband), Charlie (Cara and Luke's Son), Rhett. Seated (left to right): Isobel (Sharna and Lindsay's daughter), Sharna (daughter), Lucinda (Sharna and Lindsay's daughter), Denise (my wife), Breanna (daughter), Madeline (Cara and Luke's daughter), Alistair and Callum (Sharna and Linday's sons) and Lindsay (Sharna's husband).

Today, football provides a player's livelihood. The kids who are drafted from all over the country can fulfil the dream of becoming professional sportsmen. Their contracts are at unthinkable levels compared to the pittance we were paid, but as a consequence the players are more skilful and better conditioned. As the game becomes more professional, it must never lose sight of our wonderful fans. We must recognise how Australian Football has always played an important part in the lives of Australian families. It stays with you through good times and the worst of times. It never skips a generation. Anyone who has witnessed the game – in any era – will understand the excitement and passion it can create. Australian Football tests all the physical attributes of an athlete: the ability to run, jump, kick and tackle and be courageous. That's what makes it the greatest game in the world.

To those who built this game I can only say thank you for creating a masterpiece. May it last forever.

Kevin Bartlett, April 2011

CAREER CHRONOLOGY

Name
Kevin Charles Bartlett

Born
March 6, 1947,
Carlton, Victoria

Recruited from
Richmond fourths

Height and weight
175 cm/71 kg

Playing career
Richmond (1965–1983)
403 games, 778 goals

Coaching career
Richmond (1988–1991)
88 games – 27 wins,
61 losses

Premierships
1967, 1969, 1973–74, 1980

Best-and-fairest awards
1967–68, 1973–74, 1977

Leading goalkicker
1974–75, 1977, 1983

Richmond captain 1979

Norm Smith Medal 1980

Victorian captain 1977

1962
- At age 15, Bartlett, wins the Richmond under-17s best-and-fairest award as well as the leading-goalkicker award.

1963
- Wins the Richmond under-19s best-and-fairest.
- During the finals, he injures his hip. While waiting in the dressing room for an ambulance, he meets Jack Dyer for the first time.

1964
- Recuperates following the removal of a cyst in his hip and plays in both the under-17s and under-19s.
- Plays at full-forward for the under-19s in the finals series.

1965
Games: 14 Goals: 13
- Plays his first senior game for Richmond in round three, against St Kilda at the MCG, aged 18 years and 56 days. Starts on the bench and is given a run moments before three-quarter time.
- Returns to the Richmond under-19s for one week to captain the side against Geelong in the curtain-raiser to the state game between Victoria and Western Australia at the MCG. Kicks 6.8 while playing as a rover and returns to the seniors the following week.

1966
Games: 14 Goals: 19
- Tom Hafey takes over as senior coach. Bartlett, as 19th man, sits alongside Hafey in the coach's first game.
- Establishes himself as rover by season's end. Begins a streak of 150 consecutive games.

1967
Games: 20 Goals: 38
- A member of the team that wins Richmond's first premiership in 24 years. Kicks three goals in the Grand Final, which is his 48th game of League football.
- Wins his first senior best-and-fairest award, The Jack Dyer Medal, at the age of 20.
- Receives his first Brownlow Medal votes.

1968
Games: 20 Goals: 38
- Kicks four goals, including his 100th career goal, against North Melbourne in round 17.
- Represents Australia in the "Galahs" Australian Football World Tour.
- Represents Victoria for the first time. Bill Stephen is the coach.
- Wins his second Jack Dyer Medal.
- Despite being the favourite to win the Brownlow, he finishes with 10 votes.

1969
Games: 22 Goals: 30
- Kicks a goal in the 25-point win over Carlton in the Grand Final.
- Plays in his second Richmond premiership side.
- Finishes fifth in the Brownlow Medal with 14 votes. Fitzroy's Kevin Murray wins with 19 votes.

1970
Games: 22 Goals: 34
- Finishes runner-up in the club best-and-fairest won by Francis Bourke.

1971
Games: 24 Goals: 53
- Kicks his 200th career goal.

1972
Games: 21 Goals: 34
- Appointed club vice-captain.
- Kicks his 250th career goal.
- Member of Richmond's losing Grand Final side.
- Awarded Richmond life membership.

1973
Games: 23 Goals: 31
- Member of Richmond's premiership side. Misses the team photo because of the birth of his first child, Sharna.
- Wins his third club best-and-fairest.

1974
Games: 22 Goals: 47
- Member of Richmond's premiership side.
- Wins his fourth club best-and-fairest – his third in a premiership year.
- Winner of club leading goalkicker award, with 47.
- Kicks his 300th career goal.
- Third in the Brownlow.
- Plays his 200th career game.

1975
Games: 23 Goals: 42
- Begins another consecutive games streak, this time 173 games, which comes to an end in round four, 1982.
- Winner of his second club leading goalkicker award, with 42.
- Kicks his 350th career goal.

CAREER CHRONOLOGY (CONTINUED)

1976
Games: 22 Goals: 27
- Third in the club best-and-fairest.
- Kicks his 400th career goal.

1977
Games: 23 Goals: 55
- Winner of the club best-and-fairest for the fifth time, equalling Jack Dyer's record.
- Wins the club leading goalkicker award for the third time, with 55.
- Kicks his 450th career goal.
- Runner-up in the Brownlow Medal.
- Plays his 250th career game.

1978
Games: 22 Goals: 44
- Reappointed club vice-captain after a two-year break.
- Runner-up in the club best-and-fairest.
- Kicks his 500th career goal.

1979
Games: 22 Goals: 36
- Appointed club captain.
- Plays his 300th career game.

1980
Games: 25 Goals: 84
- Passes Jack Dyer's club record of 312 senior games.
- Member of the premiership side.
- Winner of the Norm Smith Medal for best on ground in the Grand Final.
- Kicks seven goals in the Grand Final.
- Kicks 21 goals in the final series, with tallies of six, eight and seven.
- Captains Victoria in the state-of-origin match.

1981
Games: 22 Goals: 58
- Becomes the first player to reach 350 career games.
- Awarded the Member of the Order of Australia (AM).

1982
Games: 23 Goals: 58
- Reported for the only time in his career, for striking Geelong's Bruce Nankervis. Found not guilty.

1983
Games: 19 Goals: 37
- Becomes the first player to reach 400 games.
- Finishes his career on 403 games and 778 goals over 19 seasons.
- Winner of the club goalkicking award for the fourth time, equal with Michael Roach on 37.
- Plays his 200th match at the MCG, still the most by any player.
- Presents the Norm Smith Medal to Colin Robertson of Hawthorn.

1984
- Appointed King of Moomba.

1986
- Wins Victorian father-of-the-year award.

1988
- First season as Richmond coach.

1989
- Second season as Richmond coach.

1990
- Third season as Richmond coach.

1991
- Fourth season as Richmond coach.

1996
- An inaugural inductee into the Australian Football Hall of Fame.
- Nominated in the AFL's Team of the Century.

2000
- Elevated to Legends status in the Australian Football Hall of Fame.
- Inducted into the Richmond Team of the Century as rover.

2002
- Inducted as an inaugural member of the Richmond Hall of Fame.
- Presents the premiership cup to Brisbane Lions coach Leigh Matthews and captain Michael Voss.

2004
- Elevated to Immortal Status of the Richmond Football Club.

2006
- Inducted into the Sports Australia Hall of Fame.

2008
- Winner of the Club's Best Individual Performance of the Century award for his 21 goals in the 1980 finals series.

2010
- Receives Life Membership of the AFL Media Association.

Pictorial Credits

AFL Collection
Cover, 2, 36, 53, 55, 62, 67, 70 (left), 71, 84-85, 88, 92, 93, 94, 95, 96-97, 99, 105, 110, 113, 123, 128, 134, 135, 136, 137, 138, 139, 140, 142, 143, 145 (all headshots but top left), 146 (headshots), 147, 150, 158, 159, 160, 161, 162, 163, 166, 167, 171, 172, 174, 197 (left), 198, 200, 204, 207

AFL Photos
129, 177, 180, 181, 183, 184, 189, 190 (bottom), 190 (top), 191, 211, 212, 222

Herald & Weekly Times
7, 8-9, 20-21, 24-25, 26-27, 28-29, 30-31, 32, 35, 56, 60-61, 76, 82, 86-87, 90, 106-107, 114-115, 116-117, 119, 120, 122, 141, 152-153, 154, 155, 156-157, 179, 186

Rhett Bartlett Collection
4, 10-11, 12-13, 15, 18-19, 23, 38, 39, 40, 41, 42-43, 44, 45, 47, 48, 49, 51, 58, 64, 65, 69, 80, 101, 109, 124-125, 128, 173, 185, 188, 192, 193, 194, 197 (right), 199, 209, 214, 215, 221

Richmond Football Club Museum
16-17, 57, 63, 70 (right), 73, 74, 83, 98, 115, 144, 145 (top left headshot), 146 (top left), 165

All memorabilia from Rhett Bartlett
Except 214 (duffel coat) from Hutchison family
201, 208 from AFL Collection

ROYAL GREETING: Richmond president Ray Dunn introduces Queen Elizabeth to (from left) Colin Beard, Dick Clay, Graham Burgin and me during the half-time break against Fitzroy in the opening round in 1970. The Tigers were the reigning premiers but the Roys defeated us by 20 points in a huge upset. Committeeman Ian Wilson said afterwards: "That's the last time we ever ask her to a game."

The Slattery Media Group
140 Harbour Esplanade, Docklands, Victoria, Australia, 3008
visit slatterymedia.com

Copyright © The Slattery Media Group, 2011
First published by The Slattery Media Group, 2011

All rights reserved. No part of this publication may be reproduced, stored in a retrieval system or transmitted in any form by any means without the prior permission of the copyright owner. Inquiries should be made to the publisher.

®™ The AFL logo and competing team logos, emblems and names used are all trade marks of and used under licence from the owner, the Australian Football League, by whom all copyright and other rights of reproduction are reserved. Australian Football League, AFL House, 140 Harbour Esplanade, Docklands, Victoria, Australia, 3008.

Images taken from the AFL Photos collection, the AFL collection, football clubs, private collections, newspapers, magazines and the Herald & Weekly Times. Every effort has been made to verify the source of each photo. Refer to page 220 for pictorial credits.

Herald & Weekly Times images, where noted in this publication, are reproduced under license from the Herald & Weekly Times Pty Limited, News Limited and its subsidiary related bodies corporate, and are protected by Copyright Laws of Australia. All rights reserved. Other than for the purpose and subject to the conditions under the Copyright Laws, no photograph may be reproduced, stored in a retrieval system, or transmitted in any form or by any means, electronic, mechanical, photocopying, recording, or otherwise without the prior express permission of the Herald & Weekly Times, News Limited and its subsidiary related subsidiary companies. National Library of Australia Cataloguing-in-Publication entry

Author: Bartlett, Kevin.

Title: KB : a life in football / Kevin Bartlett, Rhett Bartlett.

ISBN: 9781921778247 (hbk.)

Subjects: Bartlett, Kevin.

AFL Victoria Laws of the Game Committee--History.

Australian football players--Victoria--Richmond--Biography.

Australian football--Victoria--Richmond--History.

Football coaches--Victoria--Richmond--Biography.

Sportscasters--Australia--Biography.

Other Authors/Contributors:

Bartlett, Rhett, 1979-

Dewey Number: 796.3360994511

Group Publisher: Geoff Slattery

Managing Editor: Ashley Browne

Creative Director: Andrew Hutchison

Production: Brianna O'Neil, Stephen Lording

Production Manager: Troy Davis

Editorial Contributor: Paul Daffey

Proof Reader/Fact Checker: Geoff Poulter

Photo Production: Natalie Boccassini, Ginny Pike

Photo Scanning: Natalie Boccassini, Ginny Pike, Kate Slattery, Lynley McDonald

Photo Research: Rhett Bartlett, Andrew Hutchison

Printed in China through the Australian Book Connection

LARGER THAN LIFE: My caricature in the SEN foyer is ruckman-sized. I have been hosting the morning show at SEN since the station's inception on January 19, 2004.